Redefining Success:
Applying Lessons in Nuclear Diplomacy
from North Korea to Iran

Redefining Success:
Applying Lessons in Nuclear Diplomacy from North Korea to Iran

by Ferial Ara Saeed

Institute for National Strategic Studies
Strategic Perspectives, No. 1

Series Editor: Phillip C. Saunders

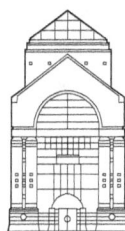

National Defense University Press
Washington, D.C.
September 2010

Opinions, conclusions, and recommendations expressed or implied within are solely those of the author and do not represent the official policy of the Defense Department, the State Department, or any other agency of the Federal Government. Cleared for public release; distribution unlimited.

Portions of this work may be quoted or reprinted without permission, provided that a standard source credit line is included. NDU Press would appreciate a courtesy copy of reprints or reviews.

First printing, September 2010

NDU Press publications are sold by the U.S. Government Printing Office. For ordering information, call (202) 512–1800 or write to the Superintendent of Documents, U.S. Government Printing Office, Washington, D.C. 20402. For the U.S. Government On-Line Bookstore go to: <http://bookstore.gpo.gov/>.

For current publications of the Institute for National Strategic Studies, please go to the National Defense University Web site at: www.ndu.edu/inss.

Contents

Executive Summary

The United States has no good options for resolving the North Korean and Iranian nuclear challenges. Incentives, pressures, and threats have not succeeded. A military strike would temporarily set back these programs, but at unacceptable human and diplomatic costs, and with a high risk of their reconstitution and acceleration. For some policymakers, therefore, the best option is to isolate these regimes until they collapse or pressures build to compel negotiations on U.S. terms. This option has the veneer of toughness sufficient to make it politically defensible in Washington. On closer scrutiny, however, it actually allows North Korea and Iran to continue their nuclear programs unrestrained. It also sacrifices more achievable short-term goals of improving transparency and securing vulnerable nuclear materials to the uncertain long-term goal of denuclearization. Yet these short-term goals are deemed critical to U.S. national security in the 2010 Nuclear Posture Review (NPR) and Quadrennial Defense Review (QDR).

North Korea and Iran are very different states that share at least one crucial similarity: decades of estrangement from Washington and U.S. efforts to isolate them from the international community. They also play destabilizing roles in the regions they inhabit, lack respect for basic democratic freedoms, and maintain policies antagonistic to the United States, its friends, and its allies. It is hardly surprising that the Washington consensus still supports isolation. What is striking, however, is the pronounced international consensus in favor of engagement, which sharply constrains an already limited U.S. policy arsenal.

Assessing two decades of nuclear diplomacy with North Korea and nearly a decade of efforts with Iran, it is clear that Washington needs a more promising strategy. Nothing short of a paradigm shift away from denuclearization is required to alter the pattern of bad outcomes in both cases. The new paradigm, predicated on strong bipartisan support, would recognize the national security advantages of a negotiated nuclear pause as a prelude to denuclearization. Allowing North Korea and Iran to retain their current nuclear capability would give them an important incentive to cooperate with international monitoring aimed at improving the transparency of their nuclear programs and capabilities, and securing vulnerable nuclear materials—the goals identified by the NPR and QDR as vital to national security.

Denuclearization would remain the publicly declared—and indeed desired—endstate of negotiations, but an outcome requiring a long time horizon to achieve. In the meantime, a nuclear pause diminishes the risk of further nuclear advances by these states and brings North Korea and Iran "inside the tent" through international monitoring. It also buys time to develop new policy mechanisms to further contain their programs. More crucially, it could open up political space in both states for moderation overall, including accommodation (vice defiance) of international demands, especially on the nuclear issue.

Negotiating a nuclear pause will not be easy. Washington has misunderstood the complex and often paradoxical effect of its efforts to isolate North Korea and Iran on decisionmaking in the two states. Because their bilateral and international relationships remain captive to U.S. intervention and veto, protecting these relationships has not been an important determinant of North Korean and Iranian strategy and tactics. They have instead relied on assessments of the entire policy context—the political, economic, and security conditions prevailing at home, in the regions they inhabit, and in the international arena. North Korea and Iran also based strategic decisions on lessons learned when nuclear agreements failed to meet their expectations. As a result, they came to see their nuclear programs as vital assets to deter efforts at regime change; improve bargaining leverage in negotiations; and attain political credibility with the United States sufficient to oblige some accommodation of their interests.

This comparative study of U.S. nuclear diplomacy toward North Korea and Iran suggests that the North Korea case offers policymakers crucial lessons applicable to Iran. It provides policy recommendations based on four key conclusions: that a common paradigm (nuclear pause) must be applied to both states; that nuclear deals negotiated with international outliers like North Korea and Iran must draw on widely accepted policy or practice; that these deals should be linked to political/diplomatic strategies relevant to the domestic and regional policy context of each state; and that the success of a nuclear pause must be judged by whether it accomplishes nuclear policy goals, not broader policy goals. Time is of the essence. North Korea's leadership transition could prove destabilizing to the region, and Iran's enrichment capability is steadily advancing.

In the case of North Korea, this paper recommends that the United States develop the following: (1) a political/diplomatic strategy to cope with North Korean leadership transition; (2) procedures for coordinating responses with South Korea, Japan, China, and Russia to a succession that could spin out of control; and (3) with the concurrence of South Korea and Japan, a strategy of nuclear pause that caps the North Korean arsenal under international oversight and conditions humanitarian aid on economic progress.

In the case of Iran, this paper recommends two approaches: (1) a nuclear pause allowing limited uranium enrichment in Iran under international oversight, and nuclear safety cooperation with regional participation; and (2) pragmatic containment of Iran that links the prospect of improved relations to Iranian support for U.S. efforts to stabilize Iraq and Afghanistan and to establish a strategic partnership with Pakistan.

At the end of the day, a nuclear pause will not solve the strategic dilemmas posed by North Korea and Iran, nor will it eliminate continued confrontation with both states. It will, however, afford better management of the nuclear challenges they present. A nuclear pause also has the potential to alter the policy context in which the two nuclear standoffs play out and to shift the political balance in North Korea and Iran in favor of moderation over defiance. This could pay dividends in many areas and potentially create the conditions necessary to move from a nuclear pause to denuclearization.

I propose first to give an account of the causes of complaint which they had against each other and of the specific instances where their interests clashed: this is in order that there should be no doubt in anyone's mind about what led to this great war falling upon the Hellenes. But the real reason for the war is, in my opinion, most likely to be disguised by such an argument. What made war inevitable was the growth of Athenian power and the fear which this caused in Sparta.

—Thucydides, *History of the Peloponnesian War*

Introduction

The nuclear standoffs with North Korea and Iran are among the most intractable national security challenges facing the United States. Democratic and Republican administrations have pursued different policies toward each state at different times, from bilateral and multilateral dialogue with incentives and/or pressures, to sanctions, isolation, and even the threat of military strike. None of these policies has stopped the nuclear progress of either state. Iran has advanced its uranium enrichment program and reduced cooperation with the International Atomic Energy Agency (IAEA). The failure with North Korea is even more acute: Pyongyang withdrew from the Nuclear Non-Proliferation Treaty (NPT) in 2003, conducted nuclear tests in 2006 and 2009, and now seeks recognition as a "Nuclear Weapons State."

Why did accords reached with North Korea and Iran to freeze or limit their nuclear programs collapse? What are the prospects for ongoing diplomatic efforts? Comparing the two cases reveals common patterns that provide clues. North Korea and Iran were motivated to negotiate based on their perceptions of opportunity and vulnerability.[1] Their perceptions were driven by the immediate policy context they faced: the political, economic, and security conditions prevailing at home, in their respective regions, and in the international arena. When agreements reached failed to meet their expectations, their perceptions of opportunity and vulnerability, and, in turn, their strategy, changed. Negotiations in both cases were protracted, and Iran and North Korea also altered strategy in response to evolution in the policy context over time—especially changes in the foreign and domestic challenges and threats facing them, and in the costs and consequences of continued estrangement from the international community. In particular, their rationales for possessing a nuclear capability expanded to include: deterring regime change, improving bargaining leverage, and achieving political credibility with the United States.

The absence of U.S. domestic consensus and/or consensus among Washington and its partners in multilateral negotiations with both states is a common problem in both cases. Strong differences persisted over the goals of the nuclear agreements that were reached, paving the way for their eventual collapse. At the end of the day, the support needed to back agreements with Iran and North Korea was never very solid.

Seminal historical events have shaped U.S. interaction with Iran and North Korea: the 1979 Iranian revolution and the 444-day U.S. Embassy hostage crisis, and the 1950–1953 Korean War and the 1968 USS *Pueblo* hostage crisis. North Korea and Iran do not have diplomatic relations with the United States as a result of these events, and Washington has actively promoted international isolation of the two states. The United States has successfully defined North Korea and Iran as outliers in the international community by highlighting a range of concerns with their behavior—from their pursuit of nuclear capabilities with possible military applications, to their lack of respect for basic democratic freedoms, to their support for states and actors seeking to threaten or thwart the United States and its friends and allies. Nonetheless, among these varied concerns, the point of entry for Washington's interaction with Tehran and Pyongyang has largely been their nuclear programs, and for good reason: these programs potentially alter regional power equations and therefore the strategic balance in ways that directly affect U.S. interests, influence, and national security.

Tracing North Korea's trajectory from manufacturing fissile material in 1993 to conducting a nuclear test in 2006 suggests sobering parallels with the Iranian case. Unrealistic and shifting goals, disappointed expectations, miscalculation, policy reversals, and weak domestic and international consensus worked against efforts to address the North Korean challenge. Combined, these tactical choices made a strategic difference. In the final analysis, it may not have been possible to stop North Korea's nuclear program.[2] However, it was not only possible but necessary to slow it down—permitting international oversight over otherwise unsecured nuclear materials and facilities, and time for policy contexts to evolve and potentially generate new opportunities to constrain the program. Prospects for rolling back a now nuclear weapons-capable North Korea are slim, but limited goals may be achievable. Assessments of Iran's program today put it behind North Korea's in 1993: Iran has one or two bombs' worth of fissile material, but this fissile material is not weapons-grade, as North Korea's was in 1993.[3] The lessons of North Korea must be applied to prevent Iran from reaching a point the international community may not be able to reverse.

Basic Premises

This paper attempts to assess U.S. strategy toward North Korea over the last two decades and contrast it with Washington's approach to Iran over the past 7 years. It is instructive to compare the two cases so that policymakers can appreciate the common missteps and lost opportunities that have characterized efforts to address the nuclear challenges both states pose. The explicit cautionary note is that the United States could end up with Iran as it has with North Korea.

Six premises underpin this analysis: (1) the United States can negotiate a nuclear pause with North Korea and Iran, which could form the basis for eventual denuclearization (but there is no guarantee denuclearization would follow); (2) negotiation is the only route to achieve these goals; sanctions have so far not worked and require a level of international cooperation the United States cannot obtain, while military force carries unacceptable costs; (3) negotiations can be more effective when accompanied by threats—of sanctions, report to the United Nations (UN) Security Council, diplomatic isolation, and/or military pressures short of a strike (military exercises, adding defensive capabilities in the surrounding region, and/or invigorating international efforts such as the Proliferation Security Initiative[4] to stop trade in weapons of mass destruction); (4) nuclear deals do not reform regimes and are not a panacea for the range of U.S. concerns with Iran and North Korea—including their support for terrorism, proliferation activities, and their rejection of democratic freedoms; (5) securing nuclear materials and gaining access, oversight, monitoring, and transparency over facilities and programs, however imperfect, serves critical U.S. interests; and (6) achieving a nuclear pause could engender more moderate North Korean and Iranian behavior overall, but as a byproduct of a successful nuclear accord and not as an explicit objective.

Summary of North Korea and Iran Cases and Policy Recommendations

North Korea

The United States has a complicated agenda of concerns with Iran and North Korea not confined to the nuclear challenges they pose. Among the central lessons of the North Korea case is that the United States attempted to integrate nonnuclear concerns into the first nuclear deal reached with North Korea, the 1994 Agreed Framework. This was a result of the lack of consensus between Congress and the Clinton administration over North Korea policy and the goals of the nuclear deal. The failure to limit that deal to nuclear objectives had strategic consequences. Washington also expected that North Korea, an isolated state and an outlier in the international community, that had traded its present nuclear capability for future incentives,[5] would act on principle and keep its commitments. North Korea's continued provocative behavior, coupled with the absence of bipartisan support for the Agreed Framework, led to the deal collapsing in

2002. North Korea recommitted to denuclearization in a second nuclear deal, the 2005 Joint Statement, but by then, changes in the policy context led Pyongyang to a crucial strategic decision: that a tested nuclear deterrent was more important than improved relations with the United States.[6] In 2006, North Korea conducted the first of two nuclear tests.

Today, a nuclear weapons–capable North Korea claims political equivalence with the United States and defines denuclearization as mutual, rather than unilateral, disarmament. However, an uncertain situation in North Korea arising from the leadership transition now under way presents unique opportunities for a new approach, especially in light of North Korea's ambitious economic targets for 2012. This paper proposes three policy recommendations:

(1) Political/diplomatic strategy for North Korean succession. The United States must develop a political/diplomatic plan for coping with North Korean leadership succession scenarios that could prove destabilizing to the region, especially if control over Pyongyang's nuclear arsenal becomes a source of internal competition. It is possible that such a plan would obviate the need for military intervention. On the other hand, if military stabilization became necessary, this would have to be guided by a political/diplomatic strategy addressing such issues as when to initiate efforts to gain international support for intervention and presumably humanitarian relief operations, among other operational questions. This plan must be developed in close, quiet consultation with South Korea. Once it has taken shape, the United States and South Korea should brief Japan, and elements that involve Tokyo should be developed with Japan.

(2) Procedures for coordinated responses/Trilateral dialogue. The United States, South Korea, Japan, China, and Russia (the five parties in the Six Party Talks) have not discussed North Korean succession scenarios, and it is highly unlikely that they would do so considering Beijing's sensitivities to how Pyongyang might overreact. However, Washington should quietly press its partners to identify points of contact and procedures for coordinating responses to events that could spin quickly out of control. This exercise could be undertaken without the five parties meeting, but a firm understanding of procedures for coordinating responses is essential.

At the same time, Washington should quietly address with South Korea and Japan basic questions related to the leadership transition, such as how to recognize North Korean collapse, and what the range of possible responses might be. Dialogue among allies will not be easy because of the lingering mistrust between South Korea and Japan, but it would be an important starting point. Washington (or Seoul or Tokyo) could brief the results of these trilateral discussions separately to China and Russia, obviating the sensitivities associated with five-party talks. Responses from Beijing and Moscow could be factored into subsequent trilateral talks among the United States, South Korea, and Japan.

(3) Nuclear pause. Depending on the initial concurrence of U.S. allies South Korea and Japan, the five parties in the Six Party Talks should pursue a nuclear pause based on phased denuclearization. The first phase would involve the following: dismantling the Yongbyon reactor; capping North Korea's nuclear arsenal; and securing international access, oversight, monitoring, and transparency over the North Korean nuclear program (based on previous arrangements with the IAEA, with possible additional monitoring measures). North Korea would not re-join the NPT until it had completed the second phase of denuclearization. Humanitarian aid during the first phase would be conditioned on Six Party consultations with the World Bank aimed at graduating North Korea to development aid and private investment. These consultations would also establish the basis for a future relationship between North Korea and the World Bank. After the completion of phase two—denuclearization and North Korea's re-joining the NPT—Pyongyang would benefit from rapprochement with South Korea and start the process of normalization of relations with the United States and Japan.

Iran

Washington has pursued different policies toward Iran but risks ending up with a result similar to North Korea. Since the 1979 revolution, the United States has not had bilateral nuclear negotiations with Iran.[7] Washington was not at the negotiating table, but played a powerful consultative role in European-led talks that began in 2003. A review of the European diplomatic effort suggests four reasons it failed. First, the United States and the European negotiators were not aligned on goals and tactics and the Europeans were unwilling to stake out an independent course from the United States. Second, the negotiations never addressed whether Iran could retain some domestic uranium enrichment—the issue at the core of the dispute between Iran and the international community. European ambiguity over domestic enrichment, rooted in U.S. policy concerns, removed any stake Iran's leadership might have had to engage in serious negotiations toward a nuclear deal. Third, Western ambiguity on domestic enrichment ended up helping Tehran manipulate the nuclear debate among Iranian political elites and constrain it to the narrow tactical question of whether to accommodate or defy the international community. Controversial strategic questions, such as whether Iran's nuclear program is civilian or military, were excluded from Iranian debate as a result. The fourth reason the European-led process failed was that Iranian elites favoring accommodation of international concerns over defiance were set back when promised incentives to Iran never materialized (due to U.S. opposition), and when changes in the policy context led Iran to believe it had a stronger hand to play.

Today, Iran's agitated and unsettled political landscape may provide a ripe environment for a revised nuclear deal. This paper proposes two policy recommendations:

(1) Nuclear pause. The P5+1 (permanent five members of the UN Security Council plus Germany) should table a nuclear deal comprised of three key elements: first, limited domestic enrichment in Iran (limited by quantity produced, number of centrifuges, and/or the level of enrichment); second, strict compliance with Iran's IAEA Safeguards Agreement and the terms of the Additional Protocol (which Iran must ratify) to secure stringent international access, oversight, monitoring, and transparency over Iran's nuclear program (possible additional measures for the assurance of the international community should be considered, including supplementary monitors, in addition to IAEA monitors, at certain sites); and third, cooperative efforts with Iran related to nuclear safety and preventing environmental damage arising from a nuclear accident. Nuclear safety talks and initiatives would include regional participation.

(2) Pragmatic containment. The comprehensive nuclear deal with the P5+1 should be embedded in a U.S. policy of pragmatic containment of Iran, aimed at promoting Iran's responsible coexistence with its neighbors and with the United States in the Middle East and Southwest Asia. U.S. policy toward Iran would be linked conceptually and operationally to U.S. efforts to stabilize Iraq and Afghanistan, and to establish a strategic partnership with Pakistan. The prospect of improved U.S.-Iran relations would be excluded as an immediate goal of pragmatic containment because differences are too great to bridge over the near term. However, the United States would signal to Iran that if the nuclear deal and nuclear-related cooperation succeed, that success could lay the basis for an expanded U.S. diplomatic agenda with Iran.

Missed Opportunity: 1994 North Korea Negotiations

The 1994 U.S.–North Korea Agreed Framework

In 1994, the United States ended a nuclear crisis on the Korean Peninsula by making North Korea a compelling offer at a moment of vulnerability and opportunity for the North. North Korea had been weakening vis-à-vis South Korea for a decade. Facing a downward economic spiral while also losing diplomatic ground to Seoul, Pyongyang had been dealt an especially painful blow by the recognition of South Korea by erstwhile Communist allies, China and the Soviet Union. However, in 1991, the worldwide removal of U.S. tactical nuclear weapons opened a window of opportunity for North Korea.[8] Pyongyang reached out to adversaries, the United States and South Korea, and as part of that outreach, resumed accession to the NPT. North Korea approved an IAEA Safeguards Agreement on the premise that "none of the NPT member countries will deploy nuclear weapons on the Korean Peninsula and pose a nuclear threat to [North Korea]," and linked this step to the 1991 U.S. decision on tactical nuclear weapons.[9]

The crisis erupted when Pyongyang refused IAEA "special inspections" to resolve suspicions of a covert weapons program.[10] The Safeguards Agreement North Korea signed allowed the IAEA to verify that all North Korean nuclear material and facilities were exclusively for peaceful purposes (for generating electricity) and to assess whether North Korea's declaration of nuclear material and facilities was complete and correct. However, IAEA inspections revealed discrepancies in North Korea's declaration as early as July 1992, when the agency concluded that North Korea had undertaken more nuclear reprocessing than it had declared.[11] This suggested that North Korea had more fissile material than it had reported. Pyongyang refused the IAEA access to sites that might have cleared up the discrepancy, rekindling longstanding U.S. suspicions of a covert North Korean nuclear weapons program.

In February 1993, the IAEA invoked "special inspections," a brand-new procedure allowing for more intrusive inspections. In order to pressure North Korea to accept these inspections, the United States and South Korea conducted military exercises (previously postponed to acknowledge the slow thaw with North Korea).[12] Contrary to their intent, however, these exercises only hardened North Korea's posture. Pyongyang escalated the crisis by announcing its withdrawal from the NPT in March 1993. In response, the United States successfully orchestrated a UN Security Council resolution calling on North Korea to return to the NPT and comply with IAEA inspections. This set in motion negotiations with Washington that would, through twists and turns (including consideration of a U.S. military strike), peacefully return North Korea to the NPT and freeze its nuclear program 19 months later.[13] In the process, North Korea validated an important strategic calculation: that a nuclear program is a useful bargaining chip with the United States.[14]

The deal that ended the crisis was controversial and precedent-setting: North Korea was promised advanced civilian nuclear reactors while remaining in breach of NPT Article III, namely, the requirement to conclude and implement an IAEA Safeguards Agreement. In effect, Pyongyang "suspended" its withdrawal from the NPT and, in exchange, the application of Article III to North Korea was "suspended." North Korea could remain in this unusual status vis-à-vis the NPT until 2003, when the reactors were to be delivered. While North Korea withdrew from the IAEA, inspectors remained in the country to monitor the nuclear freeze established by the Agreed Framework.[15]

It is important for policymakers to appreciate that Pyongyang's refusal to submit to special inspections was set aside in order to pursue the higher priority goal of securing international access to and oversight over North Korean nuclear materials and facilities. Another important aspect of this deal was that the United States offered North Korea two things it badly wanted: nuclear technology and diplomatic relations. In fact, Pyongyang had asked IAEA Director General Hans Blix for help in acquiring advanced civilian nuclear reactors and a secure supply of enriched uranium from abroad to fuel them a year before the crisis broke.[16] The reactors were an incentive to come into NPT compliance. An even greater enticement for North Korea, however, was the potential for normalized relations with the United States, which would end decades of mutual hostility.

Why did the deal collapse, given these promising circumstances? First, the Agreed Framework addressed the nuclear issue only, but Congress wanted to tackle a broader range of problems. As soon as it was signed in October 1994, Congress sharply criticized the accord, labeling the Clinton administration's North Korea policy "appeasement."[17] This lack of consensus between Congress and the administration over the goals of the Agreed Framework laid the groundwork for its eventual collapse 8 years later. Congress set additional conditions on the deal, including a call for the relocation and reduction of North Korean conventional forces away from the De-Militarized Zone.[18] As Congress attempted to dictate the terms of limited engagement with Pyongyang, the Agreed Framework was also repeatedly undermined by North Korean provocations, including a missile launch in 1998. The Clinton administration had to respond to this North Korean behavior with little knowledge of whose interests in the leadership hierarchy were advanced by the nuclear deal, and whose interests it damaged. In the absence of such information and facing mounting congressional challenges to North Korea policy, measured U.S. responses that preserved the nuclear deal were hard to justify.

The second reason the deal collapsed was that it stood in the way of the Bush administration's desire to chart a new course with North Korea in 2001 and shift from the incentive-based policies enshrined in the Agreed Framework to a constraint-based approach.[19] Many of the changes Congress wanted in the Agreed Framework were integrated into a new policy that asked more of North Korea to obtain the same benefits promised by the 1994 accord. Shaky under the weight of this new approach, the Agreed Framework collapsed in 2002 after U.S. consideration of intelligence that North Korea had developed a covert nuclear weapons program based on uranium enrichment (which led Washington to confront North Korea with the information).[20] Pyongyang lifted the nuclear freeze and in January 2003 withdrew from the NPT, citing two main reasons: U.S. failure to honor the reactor deal and ease sanctions, and the listing of North Korea as a potential target for limited nuclear attack in the 2002 U.S. Nuclear Posture Review (this assertion was based on press reports in the *Los Angeles Times* and *The New York Times* on March 9–10, 2002, sourced to a leak of this document). This latter move reversed the direction of U.S. policy from the announced removal of tactical nuclear weapons in 1991, to the announced development of bunker-busting bombs in 2002 for possible use against North Korea.[21] For North Korea, this represented a major change in the policy context, prompting a reassessment of strategy that became evident in Pyongyang's approach to nuclear negotiations a few years later.

One of the most alarming consequences of North Korea's NPT withdrawal was that 8,000 spent fuel rods were left in country,[22] no longer monitored and safeguarded by the IAEA or U.S. spent fuel teams. The gap between the rhetoric from Washington regarding North Korea's dangerous nuclear ambitions and the muted U.S. response to Pyongyang's withdrawal from the NPT was striking. It was also a study in contrasts from 1993 when the United States pulled out all the stops to prevent North Korea from leaving the treaty. In 2003, the United States wanted to avoid distracting from the case for war with Iraq.[23] Washington also did not want to set any precedents affecting its own ability to withdraw from treaties.[24] This underscored the unpredictability of U.S. policy for North Korea, affecting Pyongyang's calculation of opportunity and vulnerability in subsequent engagement with the United States on the nuclear issue.

No longer bound by the Agreed Framework, Washington acted to address one of its main drawbacks: that it failed to integrate North Korea's neighbors, and especially U.S. allies South Korea and Japan, into the search for solutions to the North Korean nuclear challenge. The United States proposed that China chair Six Party Talks bringing itself, South Korea, Japan, and Russia together with North Korea. This negotiating format was designed to incorporate the views of key U.S. alliance partners, South Korea and Japan, and to integrate China into negotiations because Beijing was perceived to have unique leverage with North Korea. Washington also believed that moving from a bilateral to a multilateral negotiating format would isolate North Korea in its own neighborhood. In contrast to these U.S. goals, China's main aim in 2003 was to prevent the United States from using military force against North Korea.[25] Thus, from the very start, the Six Party Talks have featured a loose consensus between the United States and China on the goal of denuclearization, but a strong divergence of views on tactics largely because China does not wish to alienate North Korea, a useful buffer against the U.S. military presence in South Korea.

continued on p. 18 ➤

IAEA Safeguards Overview: Comprehensive Safeguards Agreements and Additional Protocols

What are safeguards and what role do they play?

Safeguards are activities by which the IAEA can verify that a State is living up to its international commitments not to use nuclear programmes for nuclear-weapons purposes. The global Nuclear Non-Proliferation Treaty (NPT) and other treaties against the spread of nuclear weapons entrust the IAEA as the nuclear inspectorate. Today, the IAEA safeguards nuclear material and activities under agreements with more than 140 States.

Within the world's nuclear non-proliferation regime, the IAEA's safeguards system functions as a confidence-building measure, an early warning mechanism, and the trigger that sets in motion other responses by the international community if and when the need arises.

Over the past decade, IAEA safeguards have been strengthened in key areas. Measures aim to increase the likelihood of detecting a clandestine nuclear weapons programme and to build confidence that States are abiding by their international commitments.

What verification measures are used?

Safeguards are based on assessments of the correctness and completeness of a State's declared nuclear material and nuclear-related activities. Verification measures include on-site inspections, visits, and ongoing monitoring and evaluation. Basically, two sets of measures are carried out in accordance with the type of safeguards agreements in force with a State.

One set relates to verifying State reports of declared nuclear material and activities. These measures—authorized under NPT-type comprehensive safeguards agreements—largely are based on nuclear material accountancy, complemented by containment and surveillance techniques, such as tamper-proof seals and cameras that the IAEA installs at facilities.

Another set adds measures to strengthen the IAEA's inspection capabilities. They include those incorporated in what is known as an "Additional Protocol"—this is a legal document complementing comprehensive safeguards agreements. The measures enable the IAEA not only to verify the non-diversion of declared nuclear material but also to provide assurances as to the absence of undeclared nuclear material and activities in a State.

What kinds of inspections are done?

The IAEA carries out different types of on-site inspections and visits under comprehensive safeguards agreements.

Ad hoc inspections typically are made to verify a State's initial report of nuclear material or reports on changes thereto, and to verify the nuclear material involved in international transfers.

Routine inspection—the type most frequently used—may be carried out according to a defined schedule or they may be of an unannounced or short-notice character. The Agency's right to carry out routine inspections under comprehensive safeguards agreements is limited to those locations within a nuclear facility, or other locations containing nuclear material, through which nuclear material is expected to flow (strategic points).

Special inspections may be carried out in circumstances according to defined procedures. The IAEA may carry out such inspections if it considers that information made available by the State concerned, including explanations from the State and information obtained from routine inspections, is not adequate for the Agency to fulfill its responsibilities under the safeguards agreement.

Safeguards visits may be made to declared facilities at appropriate times during the lifecycle for verifying the safeguards relevant design information. For example, such visits may be carried out during construction to determine the completeness of the declared design information; during routine facility operations and following maintenance, to confirm that no modification was made that would allow unreported activities to take place; and during a facility decommissioning, to confirm that sensitive equipment was rendered unusable.

Activities IAEA inspectors perform during and in connection with on-site inspections or visits at facilities may include auditing the facility's accounting and operating records and comparing these records with the State's accounting reports to the agency; verifying the nuclear material inventory and inventory changes; taking environmental samples; and applying containment and surveillance measures (e.g., seal application, installation of surveillance equipment).

What is the Additional Protocol to safeguards agreements?

The Additional Protocol is a legal document granting the IAEA complementary inspection authority to that provided in underlying safeguards agreements. A principal aim is to enable the IAEA inspectorate to provide assurance about both declared and possible undeclared activities. Under the Protocol, the IAEA is granted expanded rights of access to information and sites.

An overview of the strengthened safeguards measures under Additional Protocols and comprehensive safeguards agreements follows:

Measures under Additional Protocols

State provision of information about, and IAEA inspector access to, all parts of a State's nuclear fuel cycle—including uranium mines, fuel fabrication and enrichment plants, and nuclear waste sites—as well as to any other location where nuclear material is or may be present.

State provision of information on, and IAEA short-notice access to, all buildings on a nuclear site. (The Protocol provides for IAEA inspectors to have "complementary" access to assure the absence of undeclared nuclear material or to resolve questions or inconsistencies in the information a State has provided about its nuclear activities. Advance notice in most cases is at least 24 hours. The advance notice is shorter—at least two hours—for access to any place on a site that is sought in conjunction with design information verification or ad hoc or routine inspections at that *site*. The *activities* carried out during complementary access could include examination of records, visual observation, environmental sampling, utilization of radiation detection and measurement devices, and the application of seals and other identifying and tamper-indicating devices.)

IAEA collection of environmental samples at locations beyond declared locations when deemed necessary by the Agency. (Wider area environmental sampling would require IAEA Board approval of such sampling and consultations with the State concerned.)

IAEA right to make use of internationally established communications systems, including satellite systems and other forms of telecommunication.

State acceptance of IAEA inspector designations and issuance of multiple entry visas (valid for at least one year) for inspectors.

State provision of information about, and IAEA verification mechanisms for, its research and development activities related to its nuclear fuel cycle.

State provision of information on the manufacture and export of sensitive nuclear-related technologies, and IAEA verification mechanisms for manufacturing and import locations in the State.

Measures under Comprehensive Safeguards Agreements

IAEA collection of environmental samples in facilities and at locations where inspectors have access during inspections and design information verification (with sample analysis at the IAEA Clean Laboratory and/or at certified laboratories in Member States).

IAEA use of unattended and remote monitoring of movements of declared nuclear material in facilities and the transmission of authenticated and encrypted safeguards-relevant data to the Agency.

IAEA expanded use of unannounced inspections within the scheduled routine inspection regime.

IAEA enhanced evaluation of information from a State's declarations, IAEA verification activities and a wide range of open sources.

State provision of design information on new facilities and on changes in existing facilities as soon as the State authorities decide to construct, authorize construction or modify a facility. The IAEA has the continuing right to verify the design information over the facility's lifecycle, including decommissioning.

State *voluntary* reporting on imports and exports of nuclear material and exports of specified equipment and non-nuclear material. (Components of this reporting are incorporated in the Model Additional Protocol.)

Closer co-operation between the IAEA and the State (and regional) systems for accounting for and control of nuclear material in Member States.

Provision of enhanced training for IAEA inspectors and safeguards staff and for Member State personnel responsible for safeguards implementation.

Source: <http://www.iaea.org/Publications/FactSheets/English/sg_overview.html>.

continued from p. 13

The 2005 Joint Statement

When the Six Party process was created in 2003, Washington hoped the multilateral format would break the cycle of North Korean provocations aimed at driving the United States into bilateral talks. However, facing protracted challenges in Iraq and Afghanistan, new players in the Bush administration's second term, starting in 2005, had taken a hard look at the administration's North Korea policy and judged it a failure.[26] A new approach to North Korea was developed that essentially restored incentive-based policies. By June 2005, moreover, Washington would even offer bilateral talks in the face of mounting concern over serial North Korean provocations: first, Pyongyang announced in February 2005 that it had produced nuclear weapons; next, evidence came out that pointed to North Korean weapons cooperation with another state; and the culmination occurred in April 2005 when a senior North Korean official told China that North Korea needed a "nuclear deterrent" because the Bush Doctrine consisted of regime change, preemptive strikes, and the Axis of Evil.[27]

Pyongyang's provocations signaled an important shift in North Korean strategy based on changed perceptions. First, the Agreed Framework had failed to meet Pyongyang's expectations of a changed relationship with Washington. That the United States was about to reverse course and return to incentive-based policies after trying a constraint-based approach only underscored the unpredictability of Washington's North Korea policy. Second, Pyongyang appears to have concluded that Washington would engage in serious negotiations with North Korea only when faced with a serious challenge to vital U.S. goals: the prospect of North Korean nuclear weapons development.[28] Third, the lesson Pyongyang drew from the U.S.-led war with Iraq was that "only military deterrent force, supported by ultra-modern weapons, can avert a war and protect the security of the nation."[29] After the Iraqi regime fell, Pyongyang wanted Washington to believe North Korea had a nuclear weapon.[30]

The fourth factor driving the evolution in North Korean thinking was that by 2005, the policy context had changed and Pyongyang was less vulnerable. Six Party Talks, contrary to Washington's intent, had reduced North Korea's isolation by making Pyongyang important to Beijing in a way it had not been in 1993. To successfully chair the talks, China needed North Korea's cooperation. Although China–North Korea relations remained complicated and troubled, chairing the talks was important to Beijing, providing a platform from which China could build regional trust for its "peaceful rise" and project its growing global and regional stature.[31]

North Korea signed a new nuclear deal, the 2005 Joint Statement, which remains the basis for nuclear engagement with North Korea. It resembles the 1994 Agreed Framework, minus a commitment to provide North Korea advanced civilian reactors.[32] Despite the return to terms favorable to Pyongyang, a day after signing the new deal North Korea issued a different interpretation of it, foreshadowing the difficulties in making it stick.[33] While North Korea recommitted to denuclearization, this no longer meant unilateral abandonment of North Korea's nuclear arsenal but rather mutual disarmament with the United States.[34] Pyongyang could redefine denuclearization in this way because it was out of the NPT and therefore no longer categorized as a "Nonnuclear Weapons State" and, more crucially, North Korean nuclear capability had progressed significantly.

Despite North Korea's nuclear and missile tests in 2006, however, Washington was determined to keep it enmeshed in a deal. In 2008, the United States removed North Korea from the list of state sponsors of terrorism after Pyongyang agreed to give inspectors access to declared nuclear sites.[35] Removal from the terrorism list ended the legislative requirement that the United States oppose aid to North Korea from international financial institutions. Yet even this important incentive did not encourage North Korea to change course. In 2009, Pyongyang conducted another nuclear and missile test.[36]

Missed Opportunity with North Korea

Looking back over the past two decades, the best chance to slow (but not stop) North Korea's nuclear program was in 1994. Despite its significant shortcomings,[37] the Agreed Framework was negotiated at a point when North Korea had a less advanced nuclear program and therefore less to give up: only untested, weapons-grade fissile material. The deal froze the North's plutonium program for 8 years and ensured IAEA access, monitoring, oversight, and transparency, however imperfect, over the known portion of North Korea's previously unsecured nuclear program.[38] It contained the North Korean threat. The accord also kept North Korea in the NPT, albeit in a unique and unprecedented status.[39] For Pyongyang, the Agreed Framework provided two things it badly wanted in 1994. Foremost was the opportunity to regain, in a big way, the diplomatic and economic ground Pyongyang had lost to Seoul. Normalized relations with the United States would reduce North Korean vulnerability by ending four decades of enmity, enhancing security, and expanding Pyongyang's options across-the-board. The deal also promised North Korea the advanced civilian nuclear technology it had sought.

Ultimately, the United States was not fully committed to incentive-based diplomacy with North Korea. The lack of a strong bipartisan consensus supporting the Agreed Framework coupled with North Korean provocations in other areas prevented the deal from achieving its specified goals. By the time North Korea signed a successor accord in 2005, the policy context had changed substantially from 1993: (1) policy reversals between and within U.S. Presidential administrations led the North to seek "election proof" accords[40] and made Pyongyang suspicious of U.S. promises of normalized relations; (2) North Korean rationales for having a deterrent had also grown to include preventing regime change (in the wake of the 2003 Iraq War),[41] accumulating bargaining leverage, and gaining political credibility with the United States; and (3) Six Party Talks had also embedded North Korea in a diplomatic process with its neighbors that, in a perverse and unexpected way, reduced Pyongyang's isolation. The talks gave China a new mechanism for asserting and protecting its strategic stake in relations with North Korea that had not been available in 1993, and for asserting its role as a rising power with influence on matters important to the region and the world. While the Six Party Talks have built some areas of consensus, they have also exposed differences among the five parties (especially between the United States and China), which Pyongyang has attempted to exploit.

The North Korea Standoff Today

Notwithstanding their drawbacks, the Six Party Talks are important. Involving North Korea's immediate neighbors in addressing the nuclear standoff underpins a strategic modus vivendi between a nuclear weapons–capable North Korea and its neighbors (China, Japan, South Korea, and Russia). Dire predictions by some that Japan and South Korea would pull out of the NPT and develop their own nuclear capability have not been borne out.[42] While the U.S. security umbrella over Japan and South Korea is the key reason, the talks help Tokyo and Seoul show they are "managing" the North Korean threat, calming public anxieties sufficiently to prevent a destabilizing arms race. The talks also allow the United States to focus on the standoff rather than regional anxieties, and provide a place to "park" North Korea during stalemates.

Despite the advantages of the Six Party Talks, prospects for denuclearization have receded since North Korea's nuclear tests in 2006 and 2009. The regime is more confident because of its advanced nuclear capability and now seeks recognition as a Nuclear Weapons State.[43] North Korean stakeholders in the state's nuclear weapons capability (presumably the Korean People's Army, among other groups) would have to be persuaded that relinquishing the nuclear arsenal would not come at the expense of their power and position within the leadership hierarchy—and that this would even advance their interests. It is hard to imagine a deal enticing enough to North Korea's domestic nuclear stakeholders, and yet politically acceptable to the United States, South Korea, Japan, China, and Russia. Moreover, so long as the international community continues to treat nuclear weapons as symbols of power and prestige, it will be difficult to convince states that have acquired such weapons to give them up.

Still, North Korea has some vulnerabilities that may mitigate the otherwise poor prospects for denuclearization. First, UN Security Council sanctions are hurting arms exports, squeezing an important source of hard currency earnings, although thus far with no impact on nuclear decisions.[44] Second, media reports suggest worsening economic conditions have created unusually public setbacks for the regime, including riots following a recent failed currency reform. It is unlikely, however, that these riots are indicative of cracks in the regime's grip over the country. Asian specialists on North Korea even assess that the majority of North Koreans, who do not benefit from private market activity, supported the currency reform because it hurt most those who do participate in private markets.[45] Third, North Korea is also preparing for a leadership transition and has set ambitious prosperity targets for 2012, the 100th birthday anniversary of founder Kim Il Sung. Achieving these targets will require significantly higher levels of foreign investment and trade that will, in turn, necessitate better relations with the international community.

"Strategic patience," the Obama administration strategy, relies on these vulnerabilities generating enough weakness that the regime will choose to negotiate. The problem with this strategy is that North Korean capabilities can grow while the five parties wait for Pyongyang to return to the negotiating table. More crucially, a period of uncertainty lies ahead as leadership succession gets under way. If this transition becomes unstable or contentious, the consequences for North Korea's nuclear arsenal would be unpredictable. The gap between strategic patience and the warning in the 2010 U.S. Quadrennial Defense Review of the dangers of instability in or collapse of a WMD-armed state is striking.[46]

North Korea Policy Recommendations

Political/Diplomatic Strategy for North Korean Succession. North Korea's upcoming leadership succession should figure more prominently in the U.S. policy calculation, considering the uncertainty over the transition, which could go very badly. The risk is high of uncoordinated and haphazard responses by the five parties to events that may spin quickly out of control. Ideally, the United States, South Korea, Japan, China, and Russia should seek to be aligned on how to recognize a collapse or succession struggle, and on whether to act collectively to hasten it, or simply manage it. Agreement should be sought on how to secure North Korea's nuclear arsenal. Dialogue would reduce surprise responses to developments that could spark a serious crisis on the Korean Peninsula, such as internal North Korean competition over the most valuable spoils of an extinguished regime: the nuclear arsenal. Unfortunately, prospects for five-party dialogue are extremely low. China continues to be concerned about actions that could alienate North Korea and undercut Beijing's limited influence over Pyongyang, and/or encourage further North Korean provocations. It is unrealistic to think that China would risk alienating North Korea, especially in the wake of a leadership transition in which China's strong interest is to keep Pyongyang on its side. Equally important is that the United States and China do not trust one another, especially on such a sensitive matter as the future of the Korean Peninsula. It is hard to imagine either side showing its hand in dialogue.

While it is unrealistic to seek to develop a five-party strategy, the United States must put together a political/diplomatic strategy to cope with succession scenarios in North Korea. This would integrate and complement military strategy, and address basic issues such as how to recognize a North Korean collapse, when and how to signal the start of military intervention, if that was needed, and the timing for engaging international support. A comprehensive plan might even obviate the need for military action. Washington should start developing such a plan and will need to consult closely with South Korea in the process. Once the plan has taken shape, it should be briefed to Japan, and any elements that may involve Tokyo should be further developed with Japan.

Procedures for Coordinated Responses/Trilateral Dialogue. Washington should quietly press the five parties in the Six Party Talks to identify points of contact and procedures for coordinating responses to events that could necessitate a regional and even an international response. This exercise could be undertaken without the parties meeting, but a firm understanding of procedures for coordinating responses is essential.

It would also be worthwhile for the United States, South Korea, and Japan to discuss quietly common terms of reference for recognizing a North Korean collapse or succession struggle, and whether to take steps, if possible, to stop it or hasten it. Dialogue among allies will not be easy, especially because of the lingering mistrust between South Korea and Japan, but it would be an important starting point. Washington (or Seoul or Tokyo) could brief the results of these trilateral discussions separately to China and Russia, obviating the sensitivities associated with five-party talks. Responses from Beijing and Moscow could be factored into subsequent trilateral talks among the United States, South Korea, and Japan. An important potential dividend would be the strengthening of the Six Party Talks process as an incipient regional security framework facilitating rapid and decisive collective action in times of crisis.

Nuclear Pause. In the context of potential turmoil ahead in North Korea, additional options should be considered. At the moment, the internal situation is more or less stable under Kim Jong Il.

It is possible that an economically stressed North Korea, determined to meet ambitious 2012 prosperity targets, having failed to be recognized as a Nuclear Weapons State, and facing a United States and South Korea less inclined to compromise, might be willing to cut a deal short of denuclearization.

One option would be to create an interim step to the denuclearization envisioned by the 2005 Joint Statement, a phased denuclearization. The first phase would involve the following: capping the North Korean nuclear arsenal; dismantling the reactor at Yongbyon; and securing international oversight over all nuclear materials and facilities—but without North Korea rejoining the NPT. In addition to IAEA monitoring, other international monitors could be involved in the oversight process. Pyongyang would receive humanitarian aid conditioned on consultations with the World Bank on requirements for transitioning to development aid and private investment. These consultations would occur within the Six Party framework, with each government engaged with the World Bank.[47] The goal would be to break the cycle of paying North Korea over and again for the same threat, so that aid is not traded solely for nuclear commitments but also for economic progress. The five parties and the World Bank would impress upon Pyongyang the realities of donor fatigue given unchanging North Korean circumstances and the competing demands of new and more pressing aid concerns.

In the second phase of the process, if North Korea relinquished its arsenal and rejoined the NPT as a Nonnuclear Weapons State, Pyongyang would benefit from normalized relations with the United States and Japan, and improved relations with South Korea. If North Korea refused to give up its arsenal, the international community and the region would still benefit from a capped and monitored North Korean arsenal. This strategy would initiate the institutional mechanisms needed to cope with any destabilizing scenarios arising from leadership succession, which could be a lengthy process accomplished slowly, over the course of a few years. It would also establish a linkage between nuclear issues and economic reform. Whether this linkage would survive the succession is unpredictable, but if it did, eventually, it could help bolster the small, disorganized North Korean constituencies engaged in private market activity. The United States cannot and would not abandon the goal of denuclearization; this option preserves momentum and offers practical steps toward that goal. A strong dose of realism would remain regarding North Korean intentions and willingness to abrogate commitments.

South Korean support would be key. The first step to determining the viability of this strategy would be exploratory consultations with Seoul. If Seoul was not fully on board, the strategy would not be presented to Japan. If Seoul agreed to explore the idea, the United States and South Korea would meet with Japan. Tokyo's support would permit consultations with Beijing and Moscow. Washington, Seoul, and Tokyo would determine the timing for launching the denuclearization strategy outlined above. A critical factor affecting timing is the May 2010 determination that North Korea was behind the March 2010 sinking of the South Korean naval vessel, the *Cheonan*, a tragedy that claimed the lives of 46 South Korean sailors. North Korea has been strongly condemned by the UN Security Council. This coercive backdrop, coupled with Seoul's more moderate tone since the June 2010 South Korean local elections, may provide the right context for pursuing these policy recommendations.

Pros and Cons

There are two main disadvantages to a nuclear pause with North Korea. First, the United States would be perceived as having tacitly accepted North Korea's purported nuclear weapons capability, which could undercut the credibility of U.S. extended deterrence to allies.[48] This is a serious drawback that would be mitigated only somewhat by the explicit refusal to recognize North Korea as a Nuclear Weapons State. Additional measures would be needed, especially repeated U.S. affirmations to allies, at the highest levels, that the U.S. "nuclear umbrella" remains in place, coupled with assurances—through exercises and high-level meetings—that the United States has the political will and the military capability to deal with any challenges posed by North Korea. At the conclusion of each high-level meeting, U.S. officials would repeat the catechism on extended deterrence from the 2010 Nuclear Posture Review, reassuring allies of the U.S. security commitment by highlighting U.S. intent to maintain a credible nuclear deterrent and to reinforce regional security architectures with missile defenses and other conventional military capabilities.[49]

A second major drawback is that North Korea could remain outside the NPT indefinitely and collect benefits, albeit limited, from the international community—an approximation of the deal it wants, minus the acknowledgment of its supposed nuclear status and the extensive economic and other benefits Pyongyang seeks. The North Korean state is too weak to satisfy basic needs but too powerful to allow for the emergence of a private sector and fearful of growing market activity outside its control. A current North Korean soap opera extols the virtues of building the socialist paradise over commercial pursuits. This shows there are North Koreans interested in market activity and that the regime feels threatened by them.[50] Establishing a limited institutional basis for a future North Korean relationship with the World Bank, enabling potential future access to development aid (if North Korea takes steps to graduate from humanitarian aid), could open up a safe political space for eventual acceptance of market activity.

The alternative to this option is to continue strategic patience with no oversight, access, monitoring, or transparency over the North Korean arsenal as North Korea moves into a period of potentially turbulent leadership change. It is hard to square strategic patience with the important implicit warning in the 2010 U.S. Quadrennial Defense Review of the dangers of instability in or collapse of a state armed with weapons of mass destruction.[51] Were the upcoming succession not a certainty, the five parties could gamble and continue to park North Korea in the Six Party Talks. However, the sinking of the *Cheonan* underscores, at a minimum, the urgency of developing a U.S. political/diplomatic strategy in consultation with South Korea, as well as procedures for coordination among the five parties.

Missed Opportunities: Iran Negotiations 2003–Today

In a comparative study of Iran and North Korea, it is natural to assume that Iran presents the greater challenge. Iran is a major petroleum producer and a rising regional power capable of threatening U.S. interests in the Middle East and Southwest Asia, with or without its nuclear program. Iran is important in its own right, as are the two regions it inhabits. However, North Korea is equally important because its neighborhood, Northeast Asia (China, Russia, Japan, and South Korea), is a region with a concentration of wealth and military power that may be unrivalled in the world. This region is critical to global peace, stability, and prosperity. In reality, therefore, North Korea and Iran both pose geopolitical challenges of great magnitude and complexity.

That different U.S. policies to address the nuclear challenges posed by Iran and North Korea have yielded similar results is striking. The United States has pursued largely incentive-based policies toward North Korea, including limited engagement through bilateral and multilateral talks. Washington has not had bilateral nuclear talks with Iran since the late 1970s[52] and only joined the multilateral process initiated by the Europeans 3 years after it had begun, entering talks in 2006. U.S. constraint-based policies toward Iran have aimed at preventing Tehran from developing civilian nuclear infrastructure on the assumption that it would not remain purely civilian in nature. This objective motivated what appeared to be contradictory U.S. policies: the United States promised North Korea advanced civilian nuclear reactors in exchange for its 1994 nuclear freeze, but urged Russia in 1995 not to sell Iran the same technology.[53] In fact, Moscow went even further, agreeing to limit military and nuclear cooperation with Iran in exchange for U.S. support for the Russian space program. This agreement was subsequently renounced in 2000 by then-President Vladimir Putin.[54]

These very different policy approaches to Iran and North Korea were also based on the U.S. assessment that the Iranian nuclear program posed no immediate military threat but that the North Korean program did. As a result, the United States pursued incentive-based policies including limited engagement toward North Korea, but constraint-based policies centering on "technology denial" toward Iran.[55] Washington's effort to stop the Iranian program did not succeed. Iran has a nuclear program today that is behind where North Korea was in 1993: Iran has about one or two bombs' worth of fissile material, but this fissile material is not weapons-grade, as North Korea's was in 1993.[56] Iran continues its nuclear program in defiance of UN Security Council resolutions calling for a halt to domestic uranium enrichment.

Nuclear Elitism: The Khatami Government and the EU-3 Negotiations, 2003–2005

The Iran nuclear crisis erupted in the summer of 2002 during the presidency of Mohammed Khatami. Iran had completed a uranium enrichment plant and a heavy water plant without informing the IAEA, which implied the existence of a covert nuclear program. From the mid-1980s on, Iran had failed to report acquisition of and experiments with nuclear materials, as required by its Safeguards Agreement. However, Tehran relied on a loophole—that it had not adopted a revised clause in its Safeguards Agreement—to justify its failure to disclose the new facilities.[57] Revelation of these facilities triggered unsuccessful IAEA efforts to clarify the nature and intent of Iran's program. A September 2003 IAEA resolution called on Tehran to cooperate or face a report to the UN Security Council. Concerned by the precedent of the war with Iraq, the EU-3 (the United Kingdom, France, and Germany) launched talks with Iran.[58]

Nuclear negotiations during the Khatami government offered promising conditions to reach a nuclear deal. Fear of facing Iraq's fate was Iran's key vulnerability,[59] and Tehran focused on avoiding a report to the UN Security Council, which would set an uncomfortable parallel with Iraq. Also, grievances unrelated to the nuclear issue could be introduced at the UN,[60] such as Iran's support for terrorism and, as negotiations continued into 2005, its destabilizing activities in Iraq. While the EU-3 negotiated with Iran, the United States pushed the IAEA to report Iran to the UN Security Council. This dual-track approach placed effective diplomatic pressure on Iran.

At the same time, changes in the region presented Iran with new opportunities. The prospect of a Shia-led post-Saddam Iraq and the overthrow of the Taliban in Afghanistan eliminated the most serious threats to Tehran and suggested a convergence of interests with the United States—a view Washington did not share. Iranian compromise marked this early phase of the negotiations, which yielded three major achievements: Iran agreed to a temporary suspension of domestic enrichment; signed the voluntary IAEA Additional Protocol allowing intrusive and surprise inspections of nuclear sites; and adopted a revised clause in its Safeguards Agreements regarding disclosure of information on new facilities, closing the loophole that had precipitated the crisis.

Why did these negotiations fail to clinch a comprehensive and enduring deal with Iran? A review of the European diplomatic effort suggests four reasons it did not succeed. First, the

United States and the EU-3 were not aligned on goals and tactics. Although Washington was not at the negotiating table, it played a powerful consultative role, and the EU-3 were unwilling to stake out an independent course. Second, the negotiations never addressed whether Iran could retain some domestic uranium enrichment—the issue at the core of the dispute between Iran and the international community. The failure to address whether Iran could resume domestic enrichment at some point removed any stake Iran's leadership might have had to engage in serious negotiations toward a nuclear deal. Third, this European ambiguity on domestic enrichment ended up helping Tehran manipulate the nuclear debate among Iranian political elites and constrain it to the narrow tactical question of whether to accommodate or defy the international community. Controversial strategic questions, such as whether Iran's nuclear program is civilian or military, were excluded from Iranian debate as a result. The fourth reason the EU-3 process failed was that Iranian elites favoring accommodation of international concerns over defiance were set back when promised incentives to Iran never materialized (due to U.S. opposition), and when changes in the policy context led Iran to believe it had a stronger hand to play.

It is important to appreciate the difficulty the EU-3 faced in providing Iran incentives, and therefore in negotiating successfully with Iran. The EU-3 led the negotiations with Iran in close consultation with the United States but consistently failed to gain Washington's support for compromises and incentives. In effect, the EU-3 process was an EU-3+1 process, with the United States as the very powerful plus one. Lack of consensus between the United States and the EU-3 on tactics mirrored the problems in the North Korean case: the lack of bipartisan U.S. support for the 1994 Agreed Framework adversely affected that nuclear deal, and China's reluctance to isolate North Korea in the Six Party Talks process continues to hinder efforts to pressure North Korea. The EU-3 were united in seeking to prevent another Iraq and committed to finding a diplomatic solution with Iran. Why the EU-3 did not proceed without U.S. support is a lingering question. While European analysts argue that incentives were hostage to U.S. sanctions,[61] it is hard to find this linkage. In fact, Europe had strayed from the United States before; some in the G-8 broke ranks in 2000 to support World Bank lending to Iran as a way to help Iranian reformers.[62] In nuclear talks, however, the EU-3 stayed close to the United States except on the issue of reporting Iran to the UN Security Council.

Iranian Media and Elite Debate

Among the most significant and overlooked aspects of the EU-3's nuclear negotiations with Iran were how important this engagement with the outside was to Iran's leadership; how the leadership feared negotiations would be used by rival factions to advance their partisan political agendas; and how media and public discussion of the negotiations informed (in limited ways) average Iranians of the state's nuclear program. Until the revelations of Iran's undeclared nuclear facilities in 2002, Iranians had almost a total lack of knowledge about the state's nuclear program.[63] As Iran moved into negotiations with the Europeans, the negotiations became a topic of political conversation in the country covered by journalists and political commentators, and discussed in the media by Iranian government officials and politicians in parliament.[64] Public opinion was not a constraint on the regime's actions, but public dissatisfaction with the consequences of Tehran's decisions could also not be ignored[65] without the risk of rival factions capitalizing on the opportunity to undermine the regime.

It is important for U.S. policymakers to understand the way in which the nuclear standoff played in Iran's domestic politics in order to appreciate the motivations driving Iranian negotiating positions. One of the peculiarities of Iran's political process is that foreign and security policy provides a major arena for domestic political competition.[66] This is both a result of Iran's estrangement from the international community since 1979 and because Tehran regards foreign policy as a symbol of Iran's continued influence.[67] For these reasons alone, then, the nuclear negotiations with the EU-3 were destined to become a serious battleground among competing Iranian factions. However, they became exponentially more important because they were Iran's first significant engagement with the international community after a long hiatus. The government equated them with U.S.-Iran negotiations to end the 1979 U.S. Embassy hostage crisis and Iran-Iraq negotiations in 1988 following their 8-year war.[68]

A glimpse of the government's political considerations has been provided by President Khatami's chief nuclear negotiator, Hassan Rowhani, a political heavyweight[69] who concurrently served as Secretary of Iran's Supreme National Security Council (equivalent to National Security Advisor). Rowhani has contended that Tehran was so concerned about managing negative public reaction to the possible consequences of the negotiations that complex questions of nuclear policy were addressed to the Iranian public. This was seen as a way to prepare citizens for what was thought would be an inevitable report of Iran to the UN Security Council, and to gain their understanding and support for the government's negotiating stance. According to Rowhani, issues such as whether to sign the voluntary IAEA Additional Protocol, or whether that would be an "act of treason," were put to the public.[70]

It is important to keep in mind that the political process in Iran is an insider's game in which average Iranians are spectators whose views do not count. However, the significance of the nuclear negotiations and the potential for the Khatami government's factional rivals to use them as a weapon against the government created a unique political environment in the country. Political insiders—the power centers, personalities, and factions who populate and define Iran's unusual political landscape—capitalized on the national spotlight on Iran's nuclear negotiations with the EU-3 to enhance their standing and weaken their rivals. During the Khatami government, therefore, Iranian political elites engaged in a public debate on the nuclear issue.

This debate was limited and constrained by the regime, manipulated to fit a familiar Iranian framework grounded in two longstanding and competing views of how Iran should interact with the rest of the world: accommodate it or defy it.[71] Controversial strategic questions —whether Iran's nuclear program is military or civilian, and whether further isolation is an acceptable price to pay for pursuing a nuclear program—were conspicuously absent from the public conversation. However, as the nuclear negotiations became a promising field for competition among political factions, and as the Iranian public's appetite for information about the negotiations grew, government officials were forced to explain the decisions and moves they made in the negotiations.[72] In essence, the more the Khatami government manipulated the media debate to deny its rivals a political weapon, the more the government became a captive of public opinion.[73]

Elite debate over accommodation versus defiance of international concerns gained its own momentum, as a result, with wide media coverage and debate in parliament that forced Iranian officials to convey and defend the government's point of view to the public in news conferences and interviews to the media.[74] In her study of Iranian media reporting on the nuclear issue during this period, Farideh Farhi describes how it encompassed virtually every key aspect of the negotiations, including whether to reject the NPT; enter negotiations with the EU-3; enter expanded talks with the United States; continue the enrichment suspension; and even whether to tone down Iranian rhetoric. Undertaking a fairly sophisticated public affairs strategy, the regime portrayed the nuclear standoff in different ways, depending on the political faction it was addressing. In the reformist media, Iranian officials described the standoff as a "genuine disagreement" with the Europeans, in which Iran needed to offer "objective guarantees" while not giving up its rights. To forestall criticism from the right, Tehran emphasized a "whole-of-government" decisionmaking process that implied both ends of the political spectrum had been consulted and that consensus decisions were achieved.[75]

What helped the regime frame the nuclear debate in simple, tactical terms of accommodation versus defiance, however, was the European negotiators' refusal to answer the question of whether Iran's suspension of domestic enrichment was to be permanent or temporary. That allowed the regime to perpetuate the "denial of Iranian rights" narrative—rights the regime argued were based on the NPT's essential bargain between *Nuclear Weapons States* and *Nonnuclear Weapons States*: that the former will assist the latter in acquiring peaceful, civilian nuclear technology. Because the Khatami regime had succeeded in eliminating the question of whether Iran's program was indeed peaceful, and because it was a moderate government that did so— one potentially politically inclined to press the question of civilian versus military intent—there was no concomitant elite discussion of Iranian responsibilities under the NPT or to the IAEA. The EU-3 stance on domestic enrichment, thus, reinforced the focus of elite debate on negotiating tactics versus intent of Iran's nuclear program and was easily caricatured as a policy of singling Iran out for special treatment.

Trying Out New Initiatives on Isolated Regimes

The European position on domestic uranium enrichment was rooted in U.S. constraint-based policies of the 1990s aimed at denying Iran the capacity to build a nuclear infrastructure. In 2004, President Bush unveiled a proposal to limit domestic enrichment worldwide to those states that already have that capacity—with Iran in mind.[76] However, intensive U.S. efforts to gain broad support among NPT member states for this initiative, which Washington characterized as a way to close loopholes in the NPT that permit leakage between civilian and military nuclear programs, was and remains a hard sell.

Nuclear "have-nots" challenged the effort to create what amounts to a nuclear fuel suppliers' cartel, raising questions about the juridical and economic implications, as well as the basic political question of who should control the nuclear fuel cycle and related technologies.[77] If Washington had succeeded in making this proposal a widely accepted practice or a new feature of a revised NPT, "no domestic enrichment" might have become a viable deal with Iran. There is an instructive parallel with the 1993 IAEA special inspections procedure that triggered the North Korea crisis. Pyongyang's refusal to submit to these surprise and intrusive inspections was one of two reasons North Korea was reported to the UN Security Council in 1993, just as Iran was reported to the Security Council in 2006 for refusing to suspend domestic enrichment.

What the two situations have in common is that neither the special inspections nor the U.S. initiative on uranium enrichment were widely accepted practice or policy, but new initiatives applied to North Korea and Iran, respectively. North Korea was the first state asked to submit to special inspections; Iran was the first test case of the U.S. proposal on domestic enrichment. The demand for special inspections was abandoned in order to reach a nuclear deal with North Korea, the 1994 Agreed Framework. However, intrusive and surprise inspection procedures are now enshrined in the IAEA Additional Protocol. Many states have adopted this voluntary protocol to provide the international community additional assurances that their nuclear programs are civilian in nature. Iran, as a result of the EU-3 negotiations, is among the states that signed (but never ratified) the protocol. This example suggests the risks of applying new initiatives to international outliers before such initiatives become widely accepted practice or policy.

Iran–EU-3 Agreements Begin to Fray

The Iranian domestic context was ripe for reacting negatively to EU-3 ambiguity on whether Iran could resume domestic enrichment after a suspension. In an attempt to break the deadlock with the EU-3 in March 2005, Iran offered to produce only low enriched uranium.[78] However, with Iran's presidential election just 3 months away, the EU-3 did not respond, banking on the victory of former President Rafsanjani, a pragmatic conservative, to close a deal with Iran. The electoral upset by Mahmoud Ahmadinejad left the EU-3 adrift, with no Plan B,[79] while facing U.S. inflexibility and a hardening Iranian stance. European failure to respond to the Iranian overture to limit domestic enrichment affected Iranian elite debate, giving the upper hand to those favoring defiance. Nearly 2 years of diplomatic efforts to resolve the nuclear standoff with Iran came to a screeching halt.

Accusing the Europeans of prolonging the suspension of enrichment and of failing to deliver promised incentives, Iran began undoing the agreements reached with the EU-3.[80] At an August 2005 IAEA emergency meeting, Iran stated it would remain a Nonnuclear Weapons State party to the NPT but also declared that Iran and members of the Non-Aligned Movement were being denied the NPT right to peaceful uses of nuclear technology.[81] Tehran threatened to suspend adherence to the voluntary IAEA Additional Protocol, which was signed but not ratified, if reported to the UN Security Council.[82] Iran's leadership also began preparing for sanctions. In a warning to the international community, the head of the Iranian Revolutionary Guard Corps suggested that sanctions could send oil prices to $100 a barrel.[83]

Nuclear Populism: The Ahmadinejad Regime, 2005–2009

A new phase of nuclear negotiations opened in August 2005 as the new Iranian government under President Ahmadinejad took office. This marked the start of Iranian defiance of the international community, often attributed to the hardline politics of the regime and the new chief nuclear negotiators, Ali Larijani, replaced by Saeed Jalili in 2007. Iran's posture, however, had less to do with the more conservative leadership than with changed Iranian perceptions of opportunity and vulnerability. While Israel continued to warn of a military strike, this did not create the sense of threat posed by the 2003 U.S.-led invasion of Iraq.[84] By 2005, the policy context had changed: Iran believed it held important cards in the face of unabated U.S. difficulties in Iraq and Afghanistan. Iran's leaders had even concluded, according to former EU-3 negotiator and German Foreign Minister Joschka Fischer, that the United States had been "weakened to the point that it [was] dependent on Iran's goodwill and that high oil prices [had] made the West all the more wary of a serious confrontation."[85]

Thus, a confident Iranian leadership confronted the EU-3 in 2005 and was about to signal that if an acceptable deal was not forthcoming, the conversion plant at Isfahan would be restarted. An illuminating aspect of this decision was the leadership's concern that Ahmadinejad's election would be seen as the cause of Iran's tougher line. To discourage that view, an emergency meeting was convened while President Khatami was still in power, attended by leaders representing the Iranian political spectrum—Supreme Leader Ayatollah Khamenei, President Khatami, Ali Akbar Hashemi-Rafsanjani, Mir Hossein Moussavi, and President-elect Ahmadinejad. This photo opportunity was designed to underscore Iran's internal consensus[86] for both domestic and foreign audiences.

It was also a sign of evolution in the domestic policy context. The nuclear issue was, by 2005, a key factor shaping Iranian elite competition and factional politics.[87] Nuclear politics had also become a matter of state legitimacy with the international spotlight on Iran's more defiant tone.[88] President Ahmadinejad decided to take the domestic debate among elites about the nuclear standoff into a new and uncharted direction, turning it into a populist issue. He began raising the standoff in his public appearances outside Tehran. In more than 30 trips to the provinces, President Ahmadinejad repeatedly described the nuclear standoff as a Western attempt to deny Iran its rights. He mobilized an otherwise neglected rural populace to get behind the slogan of defiance,[89] chasing away supporters of accommodation and drowning moderates in a sea of nuclear populism. Tehran now sought to pocket Iran's nuclear advances and avoid any major costs or consequences for having walked away from the EU-3 agreements.

P5+1 Negotiations and the Obama Administration

A new chapter in the nuclear standoff opened in 2006 with the expansion of the EU-3 to the P5+1 (the permanent five members of the UN Security Council plus Germany). The P5+1 offered Iran a new deal that included such carrots as cooperation with the United States, but still did not address what mattered most to Iran: retaining some domestic enrichment capacity.

Instead, the United States continued to focus on the international community, finally securing sufficient IAEA support to report Iran to the UN Security Council in February 2006.

U.S. strategy since has succeeded in making the Iran standoff all about Iran's compliance with UN Security Council resolutions calling for a cessation of Iranian domestic enrichment, denying Iran the ability to sue for the rights it claims under the NPT to peaceful nuclear technology. This was a crucial U.S. diplomatic victory because it closed off any potential support for Iran from other states opposed to the new U.S. approach to domestic uranium enrichment. However, it was only a tactical win, and a Pyrrhic one at that. Since Iran was reported to the Security Council, it has become even harder for Iranian moderates to justify accommodating the international community. During the period that the UN Security Council passed Resolutions 1737, 1747, and 1803, imposing sanctions on Iran, Iran's uranium enrichment capability has improved substantially.[90]

These Security Council resolutions, coupled with the failure of the EU-3 negotiations, and the absence of rewards for Iran's suspension of enrichment allowed President Ahmadinejad to expand Iranian support—or at least the appearance of public support—for defiance of the international community over accommodation. In the process, proponents of moderation—not only those on the nuclear question but moderates in general—have been forced into the political wilderness. Thus, not only were opportunities for a negotiated settlement with Iran during the Khatami government squandered, but the potential for serious Iranian compromises has been lost without altering the basic terms of the deal. In the course of negotiations, moreover, like North Korea, Iran has also come to see its nuclear program as a way to achieve political credibility with the United States and to improve bargaining leverage. As an Iranian political scientist has argued, Iran's nuclear program makes Tehran "strategically worthy" of talks with the United States and has brought Washington to the negotiating table.[91]

Why Negotiations with Iran Might Succeed

A modified version of the original P5+1 deal remains on the table. It includes the new element of a fuel swap to build confidence. There may be a hint of U.S. flexibility on domestic enrichment, with the caveat that Iran's rights to peaceful nuclear energy are predicated on its compliance with obligations under the NPT. However, this is not an explicit offer. It is conceivable that a deal involving limited domestic enrichment under conditions of strict oversight of Iran's nuclear program may be acceptable to Iran judging from the proposals it dribbled out in 2005 as the EU-3 process ended, and again in 2006 after being reported to the UN Security Council.[92]

First, such a deal would allow the government to declare victory on domestic enrichment, which two very different Iranian administrations—the moderate (Khatami) and hardline (Ahmadinejad) administrations—identified as a "right" worth defending. Second, an internationally monitored nuclear program is more in Iran's interest than Tehran may calculate. There is a fundamental conflict between Tehran's regional leadership aspirations and the distrust and opposition to Iranian ambitions and the exercise of Iranian power among the majority of states in the Middle East and Southwest Asia.[93] Despite Iran's soft power among segments of the population in these regions, the leadership in most of these states resents Iran's destabilizing support for subnational surrogates that threaten their regimes. Iran's suspected nuclear weapons program only exacerbates these fears and antagonisms. While South Korea, Japan, China, and Russia have established a strategic modus vivendi with a nuclear weapons–capable North Korea, helped by the Six Party Talks process, Iran will not have that luxury. Tehran can never erase its neighbors' anxieties over its regional power ambitions, which are only heightened by Iran's nuclear drive. Stringent international oversight over Iran's nuclear program could reduce these anxieties.

The third factor favoring a deal is that Iran has not decided whether to build a nuclear weapon or pursue latency.[94] Latency affords an opportunity for international oversight, while Iran's possession of a bomb, which would be a sign of further hardening in Iran's posture, would likely eliminate prospects for international oversight. A bomb carries significant liabilities for Iran: the more force Iran shows it has, the more it will be targeted and hedged against.[95] However, continuing to insist that Iran eschew domestic enrichment could drive Iran to take the risk. Keeping Iran on the path of latency with strict international access and oversight is, therefore, in Washington's and Iran's interests.

At the moment, however, Washington seems to see no opportunity for a deal, calculating that the regime has been shaken by the aftermath of the June 2009 presidential election, and that the fallout from that has not yet settled. Certainly, there is substantial jockeying among political elites that was highlighted in October 2009 when, facing serious domestic opposition, President Ahmadinejad tried to accept the P5+1 fuel swap proposal. Invigorated by his weakness, politicians across the political spectrum opposed the deal.[96] However, this fuel swap did not include limited domestic enrichment in Iran. Such a deal, properly packaged, would be harder for Tehran to reject since governments representing both ends of the political spectrum—moderate (Khatami) and hardline (Ahmadinejad)—went to great lengths to defend domestic enrichment.

Not attempting a realistic deal carries substantial risks. First, Iranian nuclear capacity can expand, and since Iran has greatly loosened cooperation with the IAEA, transparency over its program is limited. Second, the more the government rallies Iranians around unifying nationalist rhetoric,[97] a certain momentum is generated that crowds out political moderation across-the-board, and not just on the nuclear issue. This could result in Iran's taking an even harder line and becoming harder to deal with—especially if the ascendance of Iranian hardliners is also backed by strengthened nuclear capability.

Washington has not been able to coerce Iran's acceptance of the current P5+1 offer so far. Neither existing sanctions nor threats of an Israeli strike have dampened Iran's nuclear drive. Iran has the ability to retaliate against an Israeli strike, and both U.S. and Israeli assets would be at risk. While some experts judge that strikes could delay the program, they also assess that strikes would not stop it. The Israeli strike on Iraq's Osirak reactor in 1981 was made with the expectation that it would delay, not stop, Iraq's nuclear weapons program.[98] In fact, the strike only whetted Iraq's appetite for nuclear weapons and its commitment to the nuclear program substantially increased after the attack.[99] Iran's nuclear facilities are dispersed and near population centers, making the international political costs of a strike for Israel and the United States potentially enormous. It is significant, moreover, that, although Iran is distrusted by a majority of states in the Middle East and Southwest Asia, none supports a military solution because that could lead to a wider war. Saudi Arabia, a bitter enemy of Iran, has publicly opposed a military strike because the consequences would be devastating to the region.[100] French diplomats stationed in the Middle East believe average Syrians oppose Iran's nuclear program because it risks a military strike on Iran that would turn Syrians into collateral damage—and Syria has been a staunch ally of Iran for three decades.[101]

Since sanctions have not yet been effective, and military strikes would create more problems than they would solve, that leaves diplomacy combined with incentives and pressures. For talks to be viable, however, the deal must be altered. Further delay of serious negotiations with Iran is risky. While U.S. experts contend that Iran is running out of uranium feedstock, which limits its nuclear advancement,[102] Iranian public views over whether to accommodate or defy the international community can only harden—especially as the promise of the extended hand in President Obama's 2009 inaugural speech turns up as empty as President Bush's 1989 inaugural offer of "goodwill begets goodwill." Long intervals between negotiations, as the North Korean case shows, also afford time for expanding nuclear capability.

Iran Policy Recommendations

Nuclear Pause. The P5+1 should table a nuclear deal allowing limited domestic enrichment in Iran (limited by quantity produced, the number of centrifuges in place, and/or the level of enrichment). Such a deal would have two parts. The first part would be the basic bargain of allowing limited domestic enrichment under conditions of strict Iranian compliance with its IAEA Safeguards Agreement and the terms of the Additional Protocol (which Iran must ratify), to secure international oversight, access, monitoring, and transparency over the Iranian program,[103] and the ability to secure dangerous fissile material produced in facilities dispersed around the country. Possible additional measures for the assurance of the international community could be considered, such as supplementary monitors in addition to IAEA monitors at certain sites. Verification procedures that could quickly detect any modification to the program or production of highly enriched uranium would need to be worked out with the IAEA.

The second part of the deal would entail nuclear-related environmental and public safety cooperation that serves the interests of the Iranian public and the region at large, and would introduce a regional element to the deal. These measures would include both dialogue and cooperation on ways to enhance the safety of Iranian nuclear facilities to reduce the risk of environmental damage arising from an earthquake or a manmade disaster. Gulf states are already concerned that a nuclear disaster at the Bushehr nuclear power plant could contaminate the waters of the Gulf, desalinated supplies of which provide 80 percent of the water consumed by the United Arab Emirates.[104] This type of cooperation would address an important technical gap (safety) and produce a modest political dividend by improving "public safety" for Iranians and their neighbors. It would also build cooperation between the United States and Iran—potentially providing a basis for an expanded diplomatic agenda with Iran in the future. Nuclear safety talks and initiatives would include regional participation. Two important byproducts of such a deal could be a shifting of the political balance back to accommodation on the nuclear issue and an expansion of the political space for Iranian moderates.

Pragmatic Containment. This proposal draws on ideas submitted nearly 15 years ago by Zbigniew Brzezinski, Brent Scowcroft, and Richard Murphy,[105] who suggested the possibility of convincing Iran to limit its nuclear program "enough to give outsiders reasonable confidence that further military progress is not being made." The authors suggested that the United States consult friends and allies to determine interests and policies, how to protect those interests, and how disagreements should be handled. These ideas remain sound today. This paper proposes situating such a nuclear deal in a broader policy framework of pragmatic containment: a departure from the anachronistic U.S. doctrine of hard containment, which produced rigid and formulaic policies that offered no prospects for engendering improved Iranian behavior. Pragmatic containment would not offer any immediate prospect for improved U.S. relations with Iran. Rather, it would link U.S. Iran policy, conceptually and publicly, to Washington's efforts to stabilize Iraq and Afghanistan, and establish a strategic partnership with Pakistan. Constraining Iran's room for maneuver in its immediate neighborhood by surrounding it with states tilted toward the United States would be one pillar of pragmatic containment, aimed at keeping Iran's ambitions in check. This would also extend the focus of U.S. Iran policy to Southwest Asia, which is Washington's top foreign policy concern together with Iraq. The second pillar of this policy (and the basis for Iran's responsible coexistence with its immediate neighbors) would be the nuclear deal.

Over time, if the situation in Iraq, Afghanistan, and Pakistan becomes more stable, and Iran finds ways to support and encourage the maintenance of stability, coupled with successful implementation of the nuclear deal, improvements in U.S.-Iran relations could be explored. However, the United States would explicitly exclude immediate prospects for improved relations. Washington and Tehran have such disparate visions and aspirations it would be impossible to reconcile them over the near term. (The Iranian leadership is also wary of improved relations with the United States.) Without significant improvement in Iranian behavior, there is no U.S. domestic rationale for improved relations with Iran, let alone a justification acceptable to Israel and the Arab states. That said, Washington would need to carefully lay out the terms under which improvements in relations might be possible.

Pros and Cons

There are four potential drawbacks to this approach. First, friends and allies in the region would insist on constraining Iran's weapons delivery capability. A nuclear accord would need to be followed by a missile deal. In the case of North Korea, the 1994 nuclear deal facilitated missile talks and an eventual missile test moratorium. Because Tehran is constrained by the U.S. and coalition presence in the Middle East and Southwest Asia, there is time to reach a missile deal with Iran. The second drawback is the risk of a nuclear domino effect—because Iran is perceived (by Israel and the smaller Gulf states) as a direct threat, or as a threat to the regional balance of power. Already, many states in the Middle East are exploring civilian nuclear energy programs presumably as a hedge against Iran. However, it could take another 10–15 years before "nuclear power becomes a national reality" in these states.[106]

The third drawback is that a deal could legitimize and even empower the current regime, setting back the opposition. This is a real dilemma for U.S. policymakers and for the international community. However, Iran's nuclear clock is ticking considerably faster than regime transformation. The more Iran's nuclear program advances, the harder it will be to contain it later. It should also be assumed that moderates are no less intent on pursuing the nuclear program than hardliners. Negotiating a nuclear deal, however, could have a moderating influence on Tehran and help those who support accommodating international concerns. Getting the Iranian political pendulum to swing back to this position would be an important achievement of negotiations, although not the main goal.

There is a fourth drawback to this proposal: it would afford Iran nuclear latency, a nuclear breakout capacity. First, it should be noted that Iran could achieve breakout with or without a deal. Latency at least affords the prospect of international oversight and possible additional measures for the assurance of the international community. Even with these safeguards, however, fears of cheating would persist. In fact, breakout is more likely at undeclared, rather than declared and monitored facilities, suggesting that deal or not, the international community would have to remain vigilant. However, a deal contains the immediate Iranian threat and could be a moderating influence.

Tactics: Implementing Pragmatic Containment

Holding out the threat of UN Security Council action would be an integral part of the negotiating strategy; this put effective pressure on Iran during negotiations with the EU-3. A related incentive for Iran would be the prospect of removal of UN Security Council resolutions (those resolutions demanding Iranian compliance with enrichment suspension) in the event of a nuclear deal. Existing sanctions, military exercises, as well as the recent stationing of Patriot antimissile batteries in the region (reminiscent of steps taken to create a coercive dynamic during the 1993–1994 negotiations with North Korea) can be useful additional sources of pressure. However, as was the case with North Korea, if not carefully calibrated, such measures could also encourage the regime to harden its position.[107]

Negotiations will inevitably be long and arduous. Decisionmaking in Iran is a complex process, especially on international issues. It may be easier for Iran to pursue a nuclear program than to interrupt it.[108] Compromise is required among a multi-tiered structure of personalities, power centers, and political factions that at any given time can either be competing or cooperating with one another. The balance among these forces seems to have been disrupted by the growing role of the Iranian Revolutionary Guard Corps in the economic and political life of the country.[109] However, a nuclear deal would undermine the "denial of Iranian rights" narrative underpinning the regime's rationale for defying the international community.

Strong bipartisan U.S. consensus and the support of Iran's neighbors in the Middle East and Southwest Asia would be critical. Israel and the Arab states would need assurances of strict IAEA monitoring to ensure Iranian compliance with its Safeguards Agreement and its (ratified) Additional Protocol, possibly with added measures for the comfort

continued on p. 41 ➤

Limiting the Risk of Nuclear Breakout: One Example

Experts have suggested many ways to reduce the risk of nuclear breakout. The following is an illustrative example that may or may not be applicable depending on other elements of the deal.

This excerpt is from Matthew Bunn, "Beyond Zero Enrichment: Suggestions for an Iranian Nuclear Deal," Policy Brief, Belfer Center for Science and International Affairs, Harvard Kennedy School, November 2009, available at <http://belfercenter.ksg.harvard.edu/files/Beyond-Zero-Enrichment-Suggestions-for-an-Iranian-Nuclear-Deal.pdf>.

Limiting the Risk of Breakout at Declared Facilities

It may be possible to negotiate measures that would reduce the risk of a breakout at Iran's declared facilities. These might include:

- Verification measures that would rapidly detect modification and HEU production.

- International ownership and 24/7 international staff, which would improve verification and increase the barriers to using the facilities for weapons purposes. (An international staff would also be more likely to notice if significant numbers of the Iranian staff were disappearing to work on covert facilities.) The potential risk is that an international staff would inevitably bring some additional centrifuge know-how. This approach also adds "legitimacy" to Iran's ongoing activity.

- Limiting the number of centrifuges to a low level. However, it is unclear how much rollback is possible. Another option is to put some centrifuges on a "cold standby"—to not dismantle them, but to not keep them spinning. It could take weeks to get them going again.

- Shipping LEU out of the country for fabrication. This approach, now the focus of discussions, would be significant because making HEU from natural uranium takes roughly four times as much work as making HEU from LEU.

- Broad transparency measures, such as access to records, interviews with key experts, and the like.

Limiting the Risk of Use of Covert Facilities

Covert facilities are the most likely Iranian path to a bomb, and the most difficult to address—a risk that was highlighted by the revelation of a covert facility near Qom.

Military strikes would not, however, resolve the problem of covert facilities (if the facilities are hidden, the military would not know where to strike), and neither would an agreement on zero Iranian enrichment (since inspectors might not find a hidden facility either). The best that can be done is to reduce Iranian incentives to take this route by: (1) Increasing the costs to Iran of being caught violating the agreement. This could include increasing the ongoing benefits Iran would receive in a deal—so that stakeholders in Iran would not want to forego those benefits. (2) Increasing Iran's assessment of the probability it would be caught violating the agreement—through the Additional Protocol and other transparency measures. These could include expanded, private interviews with scientists and engineers, expanded verification at the conversion facility, and increasing requirements for reporting and access to all centrifuges, production and procurement. Although "zero" is easier to verify than any other number, the agreement can focus on zero centrifuges and zero procurement of key components outside of the agreed regime, so that any undeclared centrifuge or procurement detected would be a violation.

To build confidence in the absence of covert procurement and manufacturing, P5+1 negotiators should propose:

- Declaration and monitoring of all centrifuge manufacture and testing,

- Declaration of all purchases (domestic and foreign) of key centrifuge components, key materials (e.g., maraging steel), and

- Opportunities to interview key participants (designers, managers, procurement officers). . . .

Outline of a Limited Compromise

Here is one example of what a compromise with Iran could look like:

- The P5+1 agrees to allow some operational centrifuges in Iran.

- Iran agrees to limit enrichment to 2–8 centrifuge cascades (other centrifuges in place, but not operating).

- All centrifuge operations, R&D, manufacture (also other sensitive nuclear operations) are shifted to international ownership with a 24/7 international staff.

- Iran agrees to the Additional Protocol and broad transparency measures.

- The P5+1 implements an incentives package (trade, nuclear assistance, etc.).

- Bilateral and multilateral dialogues are established to address other issues over time—including recognition and an end to sanctions if these other issues are successfully addressed.

- The United States pledges not to attack Iran and not to attempt to overthrow the regime as long as (a) Iran complies with its nuclear obligations, (b) Iran does not commit or sponsor aggression or terrorist attacks against others.

continued from p. 38

of the international community, such as supplementing IAEA monitoring with monitors from other countries. Washington would need to tell friends and allies that there is no guarantee Iran would forego a covert program, while painting a stark picture of the alternative: Iran becomes North Korea on steroids—a nuclear weapons–capable state with no international oversight and with coercive power through subnational surrogates.

The Political Clock for Iran and North Korea

There is a narrow window of opportunity for the Iran and North Korea policy recommendations in this paper. Timing will depend on the U.S. election cycle. While both Democratic and Republican administrations bear responsibility for the policy missteps of the past two decades, partisan political posturing and election cycles often constrain choices and room for maneuver. In that sense, the best timing to initiate the Iran deal publicly would be after the mid-term elections in November 2010, although the groundwork would need to be laid with both parties and with Iran before then. In the case of North Korea, the aftermath of the sinking of the *Cheonan* should provide additional impetus for the United States to develop a political/diplomatic strategy to manage North Korean leadership transition and for consultations among the five parties on procedures in the event of turmoil. Timing for implementing the recommended nuclear pause will depend on the policy's endorsement by South Korea and Japan, followed by China and Russia.

Conclusion

Fundamental U.S. national security interests are put at risk by allowing North Korea and Iran to continue their nuclear programs in an unrestrained manner. The 2010 U.S. Nuclear Posture Review singles out Iran and North Korea as among the most pressing of proliferation

Lessons Learned (What Went Wrong)

- Washington has misunderstood the complex and often paradoxical effect of its efforts to isolate North Korea and Iran on decisionmaking in the two states. Because their bilateral and international relationships remain captive to U.S. intervention and veto, protecting these relationships has not been an important determinant of North Korean and Iranian strategy and tactics. They have instead relied on assessments of the entire policy context—the political, economic, and security conditions prevailing at home, in the regions they inhabit, and in the international arena.

- North Korea and Iran also based strategic decisions on lessons learned when nuclear agreements failed to meet their expectations. As a result, they came to see their nuclear programs as vital assets to deter efforts at regime change; improve bargaining leverage in negotiations; and attain political credibility with the United States sufficient to oblige some accommodation of their interests.

- Both states advanced their known nuclear capability during lapses in negotiations after concluding that the United States would only engage in serious negotiations when faced with serious challenges.

- New initiatives tried out on the two states (special inspections with North Korea and zero domestic uranium enrichment with Iran) escalated both standoffs.

- Dramatic shifts in U.S. North Korea policy removed normalization of relations with the United States as a credible incentive for North Korea.

- Failed expectations from agreements reached led both states to expand their nuclear programs.

- Lack of a strong bipartisan consensus behind U.S. North Korea policy facilitated the collapse of the 1994 nuclear deal.

- The 1994 North Korea nuclear deal was not judged by what it achieved on the nuclear front, also a factor in its eventual collapse.

concerns, whose flaunting of nonproliferation norms weakens the NPT and presents adverse security implications for the United States and the international community.[110] Despite these clear pronouncements of the stakes for the United States, Washington has been unwilling to invest the political capital required for a serious, realistic strategy to address the Iranian and North Korean nuclear challenges.

Strategic patience toward North Korea amounts to waiting for sanctions, coincident with economic deprivation and Pyongyang's ambitious prosperity targets for 2012, to generate suffi-

Lessons Learned (What Went Right)

- Offering North Korea incentives it wanted—light water reactors and normalized relations with the United States—altered its calculation of opportunity and vulnerability such that it accepted a nuclear freeze in 1994.

- U.S. spent fuel teams, part of the 1994 accord, provided another lens on North Korean facilities (and set a possible precedent for expanded international oversight over Iranian facilities).

- Involving North Korea's immediate neighbors in the Six Party Talks allowed them to show they were "managing" the North Korean threat, calming public anxieties sufficiently to prevent a destabilizing arms race.

- The call for special inspections with North Korea was dropped to achieve long-term international oversight over its nuclear program.

cient pressures to coerce North Korea into returning to the negotiating table and making major compromises once it does. Sanctions have done nothing to change North Korean behavior—which may be getting worse, in fact. The North Korean sinking of the South Korean naval vessel, the *Cheonan*, is a deeply disturbing sign. It may presage serious challenges just over the horizon as only the second leadership succession in North Korea's history gets under way. It is hard to square strategic patience with this troubling backdrop and the important implicit warning in the 2010 U.S. Quadrennial Defense Review of the dangers of instability in or collapse of a state armed with weapons of mass destruction.[111]

In the case of Iran, a realistic deal has yet to be offered that respects the current, widely accepted interpretation that the NPT allows domestic enrichment (and imposes responsibilities on signatory states). Even though the United States has correctly identified the potential for leakage between civilian and military nuclear programs, actual cases of leakage are hard to find.[112] Moreover, most experts believe the civilian nuclear fuel cycle is not the greatest risk to proliferation.[113] Policymakers did not focus on closing loopholes in the NPT until the tragedy of 9/11 forced them to pay closer attention. This loophole must be closed without applying new interpretations of the NPT to Iran, which now has a domestic enrichment capacity and no longer meets the original criteria of the initiative. The U.S. approach must be based on widely accepted policy or practice, and a number of useful proposals have been floated.[114] Trying out a new policy on an outlier state like Iran is bound to fail, as it did with North Korea. The IAEA's demand that North Korea submit to special inspections in 1993 sparked a crisis on the Korean

Peninsula and was ultimately abandoned in order to reach a deal with Pyongyang establishing international oversight over the North Korean nuclear program.

The analogy holds with Iran. Until the offer is made allowing limited domestic enrichment, there is no basis for serious negotiations. If such an offer were made, establishing an inspection regime over the Iranian program that satisfies the international community's concerns would move to the top of the U.S. agenda, where it belongs. Iran's incentive to negotiate would be the opportunity to declare victory on (limited) domestic enrichment. While some may argue that a deal would strengthen the regime, the absence of a deal has done more harm to Iranian moderates and will continue to hold them back—especially if the power of hardliners is enhanced by nuclear advances. It is also important to emphasize that the battle for democratic freedoms inside Iran will largely be won or lost by internal forces. The most Washington can do is to act in ways that open up political space for moderates and prevent the political balance from shifting further to the right.

The opportunity to encourage moderation is a critical reason to reach a nuclear deal. While nuclear deals do not reform regimes and are not a panacea for the range of concerns the United States has with Iran and North Korea, a deal could potentially open up political space for moderation in outlier states like Iran and North Korea. This possibility is untested because in the case of North Korea, the Agreed Framework collapsed in 2002, a year before the deal was to be completed. Those elements of the bargain that mattered most to North Korea—the reactors and the start of a process for normalization of relations with the United States—were not to be in place until 2003.

It is instructive to review what the Agreed Framework did accomplish. North Korea's weapons program is much smaller today than it would have been without the 1994 deal. Pyongyang could have had an arsenal of a hundred or more nuclear weapons, instead of enough plutonium for four to eight weapons, without the 8-year pause.[115] Allowing the pause to end likely gave North Korea the capacity to build up to eight "Nagasaki-like" simple plutonium bombs.[116] This capacity is the basis of North Korea's campaign for recognition as a Nuclear Weapons State. It is hard to imagine what kind of deal North Korea could be offered today that would compel Pyongyang to abandon its more advanced program, especially since the international community (including the United States) continues to treat nuclear weapons as a symbol of power and prestige.

The theme underlying the policy recommendations in this paper is that the most realistic outcome of nuclear negotiations with an outlier state is a nuclear pause, which shifts the odds in favor of eventual denuclearization but is by no means a guarantee. What does that say to future proliferators? First, it is important to differentiate Iran and North Korea from other proliferators because both are outlier states that have no diplomatic relations with the United States. Any precedents set are only relevant to a very narrow subset of would-be proliferators. Delaying their nuclear programs says that the international community will no longer accept nuclear ambiguity. Is this a guarantee that Iran and North Korea will not cheat? It is not. However, a deal significantly shifts the odds in favor of nuclear transparency and containing the nuclear threat posed by these regimes—outcomes that advance vital U.S. national security interests.

In order for delay to be accepted as a valid intermediate U.S. goal, as the prelude to denuclearization, a paradigm shift is needed in the policymaking community. In practical terms, this means two things: placing greater emphasis on improving transparency into the programs and capabilities of these outlier states, and on securing vulnerable nuclear materials. Both policies are already top U.S. priorities according to the 2010 U.S. Nuclear Posture Review.[117] Implementing this paradigm shift requires articulating a clear rationale for denuclearization as an endstate requiring a long time horizon to achieve. During that long time horizon, dangerous precedents and new realities can arise that put U.S. national security interests at risk. A nuclear pause obviates these risks: it permits oversight over otherwise unsecured nuclear materials and facilities; limits progress in any weapons program; and buys time for evolving policy contexts to generate new opportunities to further contain the nuclear program. In outlier states, moreover, a nuclear pause may open up political space for moderate behavior.

In the case of North Korea, Washington rolled the dice and ended up trading an imperfect but valuable nuclear pause for a nuclear weapons–capable North Korea. This history has not been lost on Iran. Delaying serious negotiations to reach a nuclear deal carries substantial costs. It is hard, and may even be impossible, to recover lost negotiating ground as these states create new facts and realities by advancing their nuclear programs. The risk of current U.S. Iran policy, summed up by an Iranian political scientist, is that "Iran might succeed in its nuclear program and reach a point that America will be unable to reverse."[118] That, ultimately, is the lesson of North Korea.

Notes

[1] According to North Korean and Iranian public statements, published accounts and analyses of the negotiations, and the academic literature on these states.

[2] North Korea has a plutonium program and has been suspected of pursuing an enriched uranium program.

[3] Iran was estimated in February 2009 to have enough low-enriched uranium that, if converted to weapons-grade, would be enough for one bomb (see EastWest Institute, "Iran's Nuclear and Missile Potential," May 2009). By contrast, North Korea in 1993 had one to two bombs' worth of weapons-grade plutonium. There is considerable dispute over this figure, with some estimates suggesting North Korea had as much as six bombs' worth of weapons-grade plutonium (see Federation of American Scientists' guide to North Korea, at <www.fas.org/nuke/guide/dprk/nuke/index.html>). The wide range in estimates also reflects differing assessments of how many weapons would be produced from reprocessing the 8,000 spent fuel rods left in the country. This could have yielded enough weapons-grade fissile material for up to six weapons according to a paper that quotes several nuclear experts. See Mary Beth Nikitin, "North Korea's Nuclear Weapons: Technical Issues," Congressional Research Service, December 16, 2009, 5. Another relevant comparison between Iran and North Korea is between their weapons delivery systems. Iran's missile program today is ahead of North Korea's program as it was in 1993. By the early 1990s, North Korea had not completed indigenous production of intermediate range missiles; Iran today has ballistic missiles that can hit its neighbors. See the Nuclear Threat Initiative (NTI), Iran and North Korea Missile Overviews at <www.nti.org/e_research/profiles/Iran/Missile/index.html> and <www.nti.org/e_research/profiles/NorthKorea/Missile/index.html>.

[4] PSI is a global effort to stop trafficking of weapons of mass destruction, their delivery systems, and related materials to and from states and nonstate actors of proliferation concern. It was launched in May 2003 and 95 countries have endorsed it. (See <www.state.gov/t/isn/c10390.htm>.)

[5] The immediate incentive was heavy fuel oil to meet North Korean energy needs, but the major incentives were the provision—by around 2003—of two advanced civilian nuclear reactors followed by steps leading to normalized relations with the United States, if North Korea was in NPT compliance.

[6] Jonathan D. Pollack, "North Korea's Nuclear Weapons Development," Institut Français des Relations Internationales (IFRI), Security Studies Center, Spring 2010, 20–21. Pollack writes: "According to North Korean officials, the DPRK's first nuclear test of 2006 and its accumulation of weaponized plutonium represented a fundamental strategic divide that reduced the importance of full relations with the United States." The 2005 Joint Statement was finalized September 19, 2005, and North Korea's first nuclear test was on October 9, 2006, a year later.

[7] A U.S.-Iran civilian nuclear deal was negotiated in the late 1970s under the Shah's government; it was initialed but never ratified, overtaken by the events of the 1979 revolution.

[8] On September 17, 1991, President Bush announced that the United States would eliminate worldwide an inventory of ground-launched tactical nuclear weapons from surface ships and attack submarines. This was prompted by concern over the security of nuclear weapons in the former Soviet Union, which announced reciprocal steps on October 5, 1991. See Dr. Nikolai Sokov, NTI Issue Brief, May 2002.

[9] Korea Central News Agency, "Detailed Report Explains NPT Withdrawal," January 22, 2003.

[10] International Atomic Energy Agency (IAEA) special inspections are now part of the Additional Protocol, a voluntary mechanism enabling surprise and intrusive inspections of nuclear sites.

[11] See IAEA, Fact Sheet on DPRK Nuclear Safeguards.

[12] In 1992, Seoul and Pyongyang signed the North-South Joint Denuclearization Declaration, and the Basic Agreement (on Reconciliation, Non-Aggression and Cooperation between South and North Korea). The Bush administration in 1991 had also initiated senior-level talks with North Korea.

[13] Robert Litwak, *Rogue States and U.S. Foreign Policy: Containment after the Cold War* (Washington, DC: The Woodrow Wilson Center Press, 2000), 198–233.

[14] Joel Wit and Leon V. Sigal, in *North Korea and Iran*, ed. Barry Blechman (Washington, DC: Stimson Center, May 2009), 3.

[15] IAEA, Fact Sheet on DPRK Nuclear Safeguards. North Korea on June 13, 1994, withdrew from its membership in the IAEA (which began in 1974). Pyongyang argued that it was in a special position with regard to its Safeguards Agreement and no longer obliged to allow IAEA inspectors to carry out their work. However, the Agreed Framework, signed October 21, 1994, stipulated that the IAEA would be allowed to monitor the nuclear freeze, and the IAEA maintained a continuous presence in North Korea until the Agreed Framework collapsed in late 2002, and North Korea ordered IAEA inspectors to leave the country on December 27, 2002.

[16] Don Oberdorfer, *The Two Koreas: A Contemporary History* (New York: Basic Books, 1997), 290.

[17] Litwak, 80.

[18] U.S. House of Representatives, House Joint Resolution 83, Section IIIA, March 30, 1995.

[19] This characterization of incentive-based and constraint-based policies draws from Pollack, "North Korea's Nuclear Weapons Development," 11. He defines *incentive-based* approaches as those emphasizing political and economic inducements—engagement, provision of energy and economic aid, bilateral and multilateral pledges of peaceful intent, efforts to establish diplomatic relations, and technical assistance in securing nuclear materials and disabling nuclear facilities. *Constraint-based* approaches deny the means to pursue a nuclear program and mitigate potential threats posed by existing capabilities—deterrence and defense, sanctions and interdiction of illicit technology acquisitions and weapons shipments, and pressure and attempted isolation.

[20] Former Under Secretary of State John Bolton wrote that the evidence of the covert North Korean program was "the hammer I had been looking for to shatter the Agreed Framework." John Bolton, *Surrender Is Not an Option* (New York: Simon and Schuster, 2007), 106. See pages 100–117 for a useful broader discussion.

[21] Both the 1991 and 2002 U.S. policies were applicable worldwide, but the 2002 Nuclear Posture Review allegedly listed a few states, including North Korea, as potential targets of attack.

[22] Reprocessing the 8,000 spent fuel rods could have yielded enough weapons-grade fissile material for up to six weapons, according to a paper that quotes several nuclear experts. See Mary Beth Nikitin, "North Korea's Nuclear Weapons: Technical Issues," Congressional Research Service, December 16, 2009, 5.

[23] Bolton, 115.

[24] George Perkovich, "The End of the Nonproliferation Regime?" *Current History* 105, no. 694 (November 2006), 359.

[25] Andrew Scobell, "China and North Korea: The Limits of Influence," *Current History* 102, no. 665 (September 2003), 275.

[26] Charles L. Pritchard, *Failed Diplomacy: The Tragic Story of How North Korea Got the Bomb* (Washington, DC: The Brookings Institution, 2007), 108.

[27] Mike Chinoy, *Meltdown: The Inside Story of the North Korean Nuclear Crisis* (New York: St. Martin's Press, 2008), 235.

[28] See Pollack, 22. Pollack asserts a close correlation between the 2006 nuclear test and the increased negotiating latitude of the United States in 2005, suggesting leaders in Pyongyang had concluded that Washington would only negotiate seriously when confronted with acute challenges to core U.S. objectives.

[29] Korea Central News Agency, "Statement of Foreign Ministry Spokesman Blasts UNSC's Discussion of Korean Nuclear Issue," April 3, 2003.

[30] Siegfried S. Hecker, "Lessons Learned from the North Korean Nuclear Crises," *Daedalus* (Winter 2010), 46.

[31] Yoichi Funabashi, *The Peninsula Question: A Chronicle of the Second North Korea Nuclear Crisis* (Washington, DC: Brookings Institution Press, 2007), 318; see also his general discussion of China, pp. 300–328.

[32] Also missing from the 2005 Joint Statement are the expanded conditions for normalization proposed by Congress, some of which were incorporated into the Bush administration's first term North Korea policy.

[33] North Korea released a statement warning the United States not to "even dream of" the North's "dismantling its nuclear deterrent capability" before light-water reactors are provided. The other five parties in the Six Party Talks had not promised to provide reactors, which had been a key feature of the 1994 Agreed Framework, only to consider doing so. Korea Central News Agency, "DPRK Foreign Ministry Spokesman Statement on Six Party Talks," September 20, 2005.

[34] Korea Central News Agency, "DPRK Foreign Minister Clarifies Stand on New Measures to Bolster War Deterrent," October 3, 2006.

[35] Paul Richter, "U.S. Drops North Korea from Terrorism List After New Deal," *Los Angeles Times*, October 12, 2008.

[36] Some Asian officials contend that the second nuclear test was undertaken to set the tone for the new U.S. President, lay the groundwork for Kim Jong Il's legacy, and leave Kim Jong-un, his successor, a nuclear weapons–capable North Korea; interviews with Asian officials, April 7–14, 2010.

[37] The deal was bilateral rather than multilateral, and it allowed North Korea to remain in violation of a key NPT provision with no clear timetable for compliance, among other flaws. See Korea Central News Agency, "DPRK Foreign Minister Clarifies Stand."

[38] At the time the Agreed Framework was signed in 1994, the plutonium program was known, but a uranium enrichment program had been long suspected. The accord explicitly covered the plutonium program and also uranium enrichment by referring to the 1992 North South Denuclearization Declaration.

[39] This was a major flaw of the deal. It allowed North Korea to believe it played by special rules that exempted it from fulfilling difficult obligations. That North Korean view was accentuated by the U.S. policy about-face in 2005—a sudden return to incentive-based diplomacy.

[40] Victor D. Cha, "What Do They Really Want? Obama's North Korea Conundrum," *The Washington Quarterly* (October 2009), 126.

[41] Victor D. Cha, Testimony before the Senate Foreign Relations Committee, June 11, 2009, 2.

[42] Graham Allison, Herve de Carmoy, Therese Delpech, and Chung Min Lee, "Nuclear Proliferation: Risk and Responsibility," The Trilateral Commission, 2006, 11.

[43] Statement for the Record by Dennis C. Blair to Senate Select Committee on Intelligence, 15.

[44] Interviews with Asian government officials, April 7–14, 2010.

[45] Ibid.

[46] U.S. Department of Defense, *Quadrennial Defense Review Report*, February 2010, iv. The report warns of the potential for "rapid proliferation of WMD material, weapons, and technology" that could quickly become a global crisis posing a direct physical threat to the United States and all other nations.

[47] See Bradley O. Babson's article, "Visualizing a North Korean 'Bold Switchover': International Financial Institutions and Economic Development in the DPRK," in Nicholas Eberstadt et al., *What If? Economic Implications of a Fundamental Shift in North Korean Security Policy* (Seattle: The National Bureau of Asian Research, July 2006), 11–24.

[48] Cha, Testimony before the Senate Foreign Relations Committee, June 11, 2009.

[49] U.S. Department of Defense, *Nuclear Posture Review Report*, Washington, April 2010, vi–vii.

[50] Interview with Asian government official, April 7, 2010.

[51] *Quadrennial Defense Review Report*, 46.

[52] See note 7, p. 46.

[53] Litwak, 171–172.

[54] Mark N. Katz, "Exploiting Rivalries: Putin's Foreign Policy," *Current History* (October 2004), 339.

[55] Litwak, 172.

[56] EastWest Institute; Federation of America Scientists; Nikitin; and NTI.

[57] Jacqueline Shire and David Albright, "Iran's NPT Violations—Numerous and Possibly On-Going?" Institute for Science and International Security (ISIS), September 29, 2006, 5.

[58] Joschka Fischer, "Iran: High Stakes," Speech delivered in Iran, August 1, 2006, reprinted in *Dissent Magazine* (Winter 2007), 2.

[59] Hassan Rowhani stated publicly that Iran thought it might be attacked before Iraq. Speech to the Supreme Cultural Revolution Council, "Beyond the Challenges Facing Iran and the IAEA Concerning the Nuclear Dossier," September 30, 2005.

[60] Ibid.

[61] François Niccoullaud, "Atouts et faiblesses de l'Europe dans la crise nucléaire iranienne," *Fondation Res Publica* (Novembre 20, 2006), 4.

[62] Testimony by U.S. Treasury Deputy Assistant Secretary William E. Schuerch, October 29, 2003, to the House Financial Services Subcommittee on Domestic and International Monetary Policy.

[63] Farideh Farhi, "'Atomic Energy Is Our Assured Right': Nuclear Policy and the Shaping of Iranian Public Opinion," in *Nuclear Politics in Iran*, ed. Judith S. Yaphe, Institute for National Strategic Studies, Middle East Strategic Perspectives Series, No. 1 (Washington, DC: National Defense University Press, May 2010), 4–7.

[64] Ibid.

[65] Jerrold D. Green, Frederic Wehrey, and Charles Wolf, Jr., "Understanding Iran" (RAND, 2009), 29.

[66] David E. Thaler et al., "Mullahs, Guards, and Bonyads" (RAND, 2010), 76–78.

[67] Ibid., 102.

[68] Chen Kane, "Nuclear Decision-Making in Iran: A Rare Glimpse," *Middle East Brief*, no. 5 (May 2006).

[69] Thaler et al., 88.

[70] Hassan Rowhani, Speech to the Supreme Cultural Revolution Council: "Beyond the Challenges Facing Iran and the IAEA Concerning the Nuclear Dossier," September 30, 2005 (this speech may have been delivered in 2004, but published in 2005).

[71] See Shahram Chubin, "The Iranian Nuclear Riddle After June 12," *The Washington Quarterly* (January 2010), 164. Chubin says Iran's nuclear policy has never been publicly debated and that the accommodation vs. defiance debate is a surrogate for a broader question: how should Iran relate to the international community.

[72] Farhi, 5.

[73] Green et al., 30.

[74] Farhi, 7, 9.

[75] Ibid., 7, 10.

[76] President George W. Bush, speech on "Weapons of Mass Destruction Proliferation," February 11, 2004, at National Defense University, Washington, DC. See <politicallibrary.net>.

[77] Sean Lucas, "The Bush Proposals: A Global Strategy for Combating the Spread of Nuclear Weapons Technology or a Sanctioned Nuclear Cartel?" Center for Nonproliferation Studies, Monterey Institute of International Studies, November 2004.

[78] Peter Crail, "History of Official Proposals on the Iranian Nuclear Issue," Arms Control Association. It should be noted that the ability to produce low-enriched uranium, however, presumes an eventual ability to produce weapons-grade uranium by further enrichment.

[79] Entretien avec Bruno Tertrais, Fondation Robert Schuman, European Interview No. 8, July 17, 2006.

[80] International Atomic Energy Agency, INFCIRC/648, 1 August 2005, "Communication dated 1 August 2005 received from the Permanent Mission of the Islamic Republic of Iran to the Agency."

[81] Sirus Naseri, "Iran's Statement at IAEA Emergency Meeting," Statement, Mehr News Agency, August 10, 2005.

[82] Farhi, 13.

[83] AFX News Ltd, "Iran Says Sanctions Could Push Oil to 100 USD/barrel," Forbes.com, September 23, 2005.

[84] Asian diplomats, interviewed April 7–14, 2010, even assess that Iran does not take the Israeli threat seriously.

[85] Joschka Fischer, "The Case for Bargaining with Iran," *The Washington Post*, May 29, 2006.

[86] Farhi, 12.

[87] Thaler et al., 92.

[88] Ibid., 96.

[89] Ibid., 97.

[90] Liming Hua, "Iran Offers the US a Learning Experience," Op-Ed in *China Daily*, March 2, 2010; Ambassador Hua is a former Chinese Ambassador to Iran.

[91] Kayhan Barzegar, "Possible Way for U.S.-Iran Strategic Talks," Tabnak Professional News Site, December 6, 2009, at <http://www.tabnak.ir/en/>.

[92] Crail.

[93] Assemblée Nationale Française, Rapport d'Information sur "Iran et équilibre géopolitique au Moyen-Orient," Janvier 30, 2008, 30–38.

[94] Testimony by Dennis C. Blair, to Senate Select Committee on Intelligence, February 2010, 13. Blair testified: "We continue to assess Iran is keeping open the option to develop nuclear weapons in part by developing various nuclear capabilities that bring it closer to being able to produce such weapons, should it choose to do so. We do not know, however, if Iran will eventually decide to build nuclear weapons."

[95] Anthony H. Cordesman, "Iran as a Nuclear Weapons Power," Center for Strategic and International Studies, December 15, 2009, 13.

[96] Michael Slackman, "Iran's Politics Stand in the Way of a Nuclear Deal," *The New York Times*, November 3, 2009.

[97] Farhi, 16.

[98] Whitney Raas and Austin Long, "Osirak Redux? Assessing Israeli Capabilities to Destroy Iranian Nuclear Facilities," MIT Security Studies Program Working Paper, 10, 31, available at <http://web.mit.edu/ssp/Publications/working_papers/wp_06-1pdf>.

[99] Dan Reiter, "Preventive Attacks Against Nuclear Programs and the 'Success' at Osiraq," *Nonproliferation Review* 12, no. 2 (July 2005), 361. This is a well-sourced critique that includes material from former Iraqi nuclear scientists.

[100] P.K. Abdul Ghafour, "Naif Calls for Peaceful Solution to Iran Crisis," Arab news.com, March 1, 2010.

[101] Assemblée Nationale Française, Rapport d'Information sur "Iran et équilibre géopolitique au Moyen-Orient," Janvier 30, 2008, 30.

[102] David Albright, Jacqueline Shire, and Paul Brannan, "Is Iran Running Out of Yellowcake," ISIS Report, February 11, 2009, 1–7.

[103] There is no guarantee that the entire program would ever become fully known.

[104] Assemblée Nationale Française, Rapport d'Information sur "Iran et équilibre géopolitique au Moyen-Orient," Janvier 30, 2008, 28. The report notes: «Les Emiriens, comme les Bahreïniens, sont inquiets non seulement de la dimension militaire du programme nucléaire iranienne, mais aussi de son volet civil car ils craignent les conséquences qu'aurait une contamination des eaux du Golfe provoquée par un accident a la centrale de Bousher, sur leur approvisionnement en eau, environ 80% de l'eau consommée aux Emirats provenant du dessalement de l'eau de mer.»

[105] Zbigniew Brzezinski, Brent Scowcroft, and Richard Murphy, "Differentiated Containment: Policy Toward Iraq and Iran," *Foreign Affairs* 76, no. 3 (May/June 1997), 28.

[106] Mark Fitzpatrick, Testimony to the Senate Foreign Relations Committee, March 3, 2009.

[107] During negotiations with North Korea between 1993 and 1994, the United States moved equipment into the region, including Patriot antimissile batteries, and conducted a military exercise, Team Spirit. Many experts believe Team Spirit prompted North Korea's March 1993 NPT withdrawal, and that a deal might have been reached sooner without the military pressure.

[108] Assemblée Nationale Française, Rapport d'Information sur "Iran et équilibre géopolitique au Moyen-Orient," Janvier 30, 2008, 38.

[109] Thaler et al., 120–122.

[110] *Nuclear Posture Review Report*, iv.

[111] *Quadrennial Defense Review Report*, iv.

[112] Mary Beth Nikitin, Anthony Andrews, and Mark Holt, "Managing the Nuclear Fuel Cycle: Policy Implications of Expanding Global Access to Nuclear Power," Congressional Research Service, March 5, 2010, 1–2. This article refers to the sale of sensitive technology and equipment related to uranium enrichment by Pakistani nuclear scientist A.Q. Khan to Libya, Iran, and North Korea. However, as the article also notes, this technology can be used to make "fuel for nuclear power and research reactors, or to make fissile material for nuclear weapons."

[113] According to a conference convened in April 2005 by the U.S. Government–owned, contractor-operated, Sandia National Labs. The conference findings were published in *International Security News* 5, no. 2 (December 2005); see especially p. 6, which lists the key judgments of the conference.

[114] There are several proposals and recommendations already in the public domain, including those in Thomas R. Pickering, Jim Walsh, and William Luers, "How to Deal with Iran," *The New York Review of Books*, February 12, 2009. For a good discussion of the issues, see also Nikitin et al.

[115] Siegfried S. Hecker, "Lessons Learned from the North Korean Nuclear Crises," *Daedalus* (Winter 2010), 47–48. Hecker is Director Emeritus of the Los Alamos National Labs.

[116] Ibid., 47.

[117] *Nuclear Posture Review Report*, vi and vii.

[118] Kayhan Barzegar, "Possible Way for U.S.-Iran Strategic Talks," Tabnak Professional News Site, December 6, 2009, at <http://www.tabnak.ir/en/>.

Acknowledgments

First and foremost, I thank my mother, Raushan Ara Saeed, and my younger sister, Faiza Jahan-Ara Saeed, who consistently challenge me to probe more deeply and inspire me to broaden my intellectual horizons. It is always important to have colleagues (and former bosses) to bounce ideas off of, and I had many. I will not name those from government (currently serving and former officials), but their constructive comments on multiple drafts of the paper helped me shape and refine it. My colleagues at the Institute for National Strategic Studies provided valuable critiques, in particular, Christopher J. Lamb, Phillip C. Saunders, James J. Przystup, Judith S. Yaphe, Gregory L. Schulte, Mark E. Redden, Michael P. Hughes, W. Seth Carus, and T.X. Hammes, as well as Alireza Nader at RAND. Jim Przystup deserves special thanks for being an excellent sounding board throughout the research and writing of the paper. He is a wonderful colleague and friend. Nicole Stockhausen, my Research Assistant, helped me think through the main points of the study and was exceptional at digging out relevant resources. Isaac Kardon provided useful editorial advice on the first draft of the paper. Jennifer Ho, who came into the project later as an Intern, has proven to be a skillful editor and researcher.

About the Author

Ferial Ara Saeed is an American diplomat on detail from the State Department to the Institute for National Strategic Studies. She was Deputy Director of the State Department's Korea Desk from 2001 to 2004. North Asia is her primary area of diplomatic expertise, especially U.S. foreign policy toward China, Japan, and the Korean Peninsula. She has served on the China and Japan Desks at the State Department, at the U.S. Embassy in Tokyo, and on the Asian Affairs staff of the National Security Council. Early in her diplomatic career, she had assignments to the Middle East, and she covered Iran as an analyst in the Bureau of Intelligence and Research. Ms. Saeed's academic background is in the Middle East and Southwest Asia. She holds an M.A. in International Affairs from Columbia University, and a B.A. in Political Science and Anthropology from the University of California at Berkeley.